Vinyl Graphics How-to

Larry Mitchell

ST publications inc.
Cincinnati, Ohio USA

The chapters of this book originally appeared in
Signs of the Times, world leader in sign information since 1906.

Please direct all correspondence to:
ST Publications Book Division
407 Gilbert Avenue
Cincinnati, Ohio 45202
U.S.A.

To contact the author:
Larry Mitchell Productions
5720 McKinley Drive
Garden Valley, California 95633

Book and cover design by Magno Relojo, Jr.

Cover and Introduction photographs of Larry Mitchell courtesy of Gerber Scientific Products

Photograph of GridView Aligning System courtesy of GridView Ltd.

Printed in the United States of America

5 4 3 2

ISBN 0-944094-13-9

Contents

Introduction

LARRY MITCHELL has built a highly successful career in vinyl graphics. He has managed this by first adapting to, then creating a few innovations in the industry. He believes that evolving with these changes is essential to growing a vinyl graphics business.

For Mitchell, if you don't adapt, you're standing still. Or worse, going backward. "I've had guys in front of me that just had an attitude. They had 15 years in the business, but essentially it was one year's experience repeated 15 times," he says. "They got to the point where, after a year, they figured they knew it all. Nobody could ever teach them anything. That's the worst attitude you can have in a creative, custom-product business like we're involved in."

It's 1976. Mitchell and a co-worker have cornered the vinyl-repair market in Memphis, Tennessee. The automotive aftermarket, he finds out, is a good gig, and Mitchell makes a good living. In 1977 he starts striping vehicles with vinyl. He's so successful that the company he works for, Trim-Line, asks him to move on up to the east side of Oklahoma.

So Mitchell moved from the vinyl-repair business to the vinyl-striping business. The work was steady; business boomed in Oklahoma. Then one day, someone asked him to duplicate a roadrunner graphic from a license plate. If the request seems easy today, remember, this was 1979 BC, (Before Computers), the days of die-cut letters, pre-spaced legends and flat-bed plotters. In those days, vinyl was for seat cushions and record albums.

"No one would tackle the project, and I basically recreated it in colors of vinyl different than the plate colors," says Mitchell. "And they matched the stripe pattern." Consequently, Mitchell evolved further to graphic applications. "I realized that we could do anything with vinyl that we would with other processes as far as creating different shapes."

Thus, one of the original vinyl signshops was born. The first-generation business involved lots of experimentation. The stripe-and-trim business was a part of the mix, but so too was a business using pre-spaced lettering and die-cut components, all offset by hand-cut logo work.

The new development in graphic design logically led to the formation of a new business. Eventually, Mitchell sold his Trim-Line distributorship and incorporated under the name Vector Signs and Stripes. In the meantime, he attended various tradeshows and continued learning about his newfound craft. In Oklahoma, Mitchell had a hot business, but the winter weather was cold for an outside installer.

Florida, with its warm outside work, beckoned. So, in 1985, it was time to move to Mitchell's favorite part of Florida, the west coast in the St. Petersburg/Clearwater area.

Another big move occurred internally; Mitchell, who had been outsourcing his vinyl work, purchased his first CAS equipment and began wholesaling design and graphic work. For the first seven months, he and his wife worked out of a two-room apartment in St. Petersburg.

Too much work and too little space prompted another move to Palm Harbor, where he had a bigger signshop (read: garage) with a new name from an old idea: Trim Team.

Speed and skill

At Palm Harbor, Mitchell could install with the speed of the best, and he could get a better price than almost anyone else. At truck dealerships, Mitchell could charge $125 for a custom-striping job that required 20-45 minutes. The dealers, who marked up his work about 300%, were more than willing to pay the price.

Mitchell's work was clean, and the designs were tight because he used pre-cut vinyl graphics, and he never cut into the paint job. The dealerships loved the mark-up of $389 to $429.95 per vehicle. "It was a way for the dealership to create profit in the negotiating range," says Mitchell. "They looked to distinguish their merchandise from what their competition had to offer."

And Mitchell could deliver. He could also install with the best of

Larry Mitchell, a pioneer in vinyl graphics.

them. One long high-paying day, he did 70 vehicles. Even so, Mitchell claims it was not the quantity of jobs that he went after, but the quality of the work. "I didn't hurt the other sign-shops," he says. "I didn't try to get their volume. I was doing distinctive, creative work so I could go and make more money off five trucks a week on that lot than the other guy could make off of 25."

The key to the higher prices is good design, believes Mitchell. Because he sold "exclusive originals" and not "cheap copies," Mitchell was able to charge two to three times more for his work than the competition.

He thrives by evaluating his own market. He doesn't sell against others; he sells what his market will bear. This marketing strategy, he believes, distinguishes him "from 95% of the trade."

"My whole marketing plan is not based on the cost of materials," says Mitchell. "Nor is it based on what the competition is charging. It's based on the perceived value of my work. A lot of guys can manipulate the striping as well as I can," he says. "But, when it comes to that part of the graphic that really catches the eye, I invested a long time ago in technology that would produce a much nicer, cleaner job."

Mitchell's first CAS system could produce work more quickly than what he calls "antiquated-production methods." His system was as easy to operate as an automated teller machine, he confesses. Nevertheless, Mitchell developed a knack of producing work others could not. He quickly learned to manipulate the equipment to his advantage. Others often told him a design (that he had just created), was impossible to do on the machine he used.

Time to move on

Despite his Palm Harbor success, Mitchell decided to move on again. (Apparently, a fussy neighbor did not like the daily UPS trucks at the house or his steady stream of customers.) Perhaps he had become a victim of his success. He needed, wanted and wished time to develop some ideas percolating in his brain. He had developed the ability to install a VOC-compliant spray-in-bedliner system for trucks that required no special spray booths or created any health concerns. Another Mitchell idea — a gold-plating system on automotive emblems — showed promise. Neither of these vehicle accessory items, Mitchell decided, was quite ready for market.

In 1993, Mitchell took out a lease with an option to buy on a place in Fort Pierce (located on Florida's east coast). As usual, Mitchell's new shop name was a variation on previous themes: it was called Signs and Stripes. In a matter of months, Mitchell had just about equaled the dollar volume he was doing in Palm Harbor. Fort Pierce might have been a place for Mitchell to stay a while, if the winds of fate (Hurricane Andrew) had not decimated the insurance industry's ability to cover his property affordably.

Fate intervened in other ways when Mitchell started a rough working idea of a new product: an interior auto-decorating system that uses a heat-transfer system to place cloth applications on head-rests, seats, door panels and other types of upholstery. Mitchell called the process (and his subsequent company) Art-A-Tac™.

As is Mitchell's way, his new product built upon what he already knew. It required much of the same equipment he already owned; it dovetailed into industries he already had worked in (auto accessory and graphic arts), and it allowed Mitchell to out-source his primary source of income over the years: his design capabilities. The only difference with Art-A-Tac was a cloth substrate instead of vinyl.

Believing Art-A-Tac to be a "winner," Mitchell began bringing it to market. Developed over a few months, the process was unveiled in January 1994. Approximately 100 authorized dealers have signed up for what Mitchell describes as a "business in a box," including uphol-sters, sign and graphic firms, auto aftermarket companies, etc. A start-up kit, which includes tools and manuals, costs $795.

New horizons

With a new business to focus on and an uninsurable business location, Mitchell once again sought another place in the sun. This time, he traded the beach for the mountains: Mitchell set up a rural shop, with the Sierra's as his backdrop situated a few hours from San Francisco — Garden Valley, California.

For Mitchell, moving on is a state of mind, a journey to excellence, a continual experimentation based on the need to improve.

As with almost anything worth-while, the journey does not come without a major investment in time, determination and effort.

"One of the biggest problems with our craft is that people don't under-stand what mastery means," says Mitchell. "What they have to do. What price they have to pay. What mindset they need to have."

Now living in Garden Valley, Mitchell represents some specialized products, such as SignGold™, which he can distribute to his Art-A-Tac dealers. In addition, he is working on a book and has produced three videos.

This book will help you "master the principles" of professional vinyl graphics installation. It could be one of the best investment in your busi-ness you'll ever make.

People from around the world know who Larry Mitchell is and call him constantly. Clearly, his reputation has spread. The world rests at the feet of a man who lives in the country and doesn't even have a sign out front.

Bill Dorsey

Tools and Techniques

TOOLBOX
(Photos on pages 6 and 7)

1) Masking tools: Mask dispensers, applicators, squeegees.

2) Preparation tools: Tar, wax and grease remover; water; Bon Ami; towels; heat gun; and extension cord.

3) Layout tools: Tape measure, Stabilo, 1/4- to 3/4-in. masking tape, 1/4-in. fine line tape, GridView.

4) Application tools: Plastic, rubber and nylon squeegees; rubber roller; surface-conforming squeegee/rivet brush; application fluid; towels; Olfa knife and stainless-steel blades; and slitter.

5) Removal tools: Heat gun, Li'l Chiseler, adhesive remover, towels.

VINYL SELECTION
Master Principle: Use the right vinyl to meet the demands of the job regardless of cost. Substituting cheaper materials is a false economy.

Use, environmental exposure and customer expectation will determine which film product to select. Keep in mind that customers shopping for lowest price will verbally minimize the expected usage for the vinyl-graphic product and mentally expect the longest usage. Select a product that will out-perform either expectation.

Manufacturing methods for vinyl differ and create inherent performance imitations. Calendered vinyl will not perform identically because of these built-in "genetic" boundaries.

These conditions outline the proper vinyl selection.

Condition 1: Outdoor usage, long-term expectation, flexible substrates (banners, magnetic signs, awnings, vinyl wheel covers, etc.), textured substrates (concrete, brick, stucco, "vinylized" canvas, etc.), compound curves, vehicle exteriors, exposure to UV, temperature extremes and petro-chemicals (solvents, gasoline, finish products). *Select:* High-performance cast vinyl if one or a combination of these conditions exist.

Condition 2: Indoor usage, temporary expectation, flat substrates, protected from exposure to UV light, temperature extremes and petrochemicals. *Select:* High- or intermediate-

Masking tools.

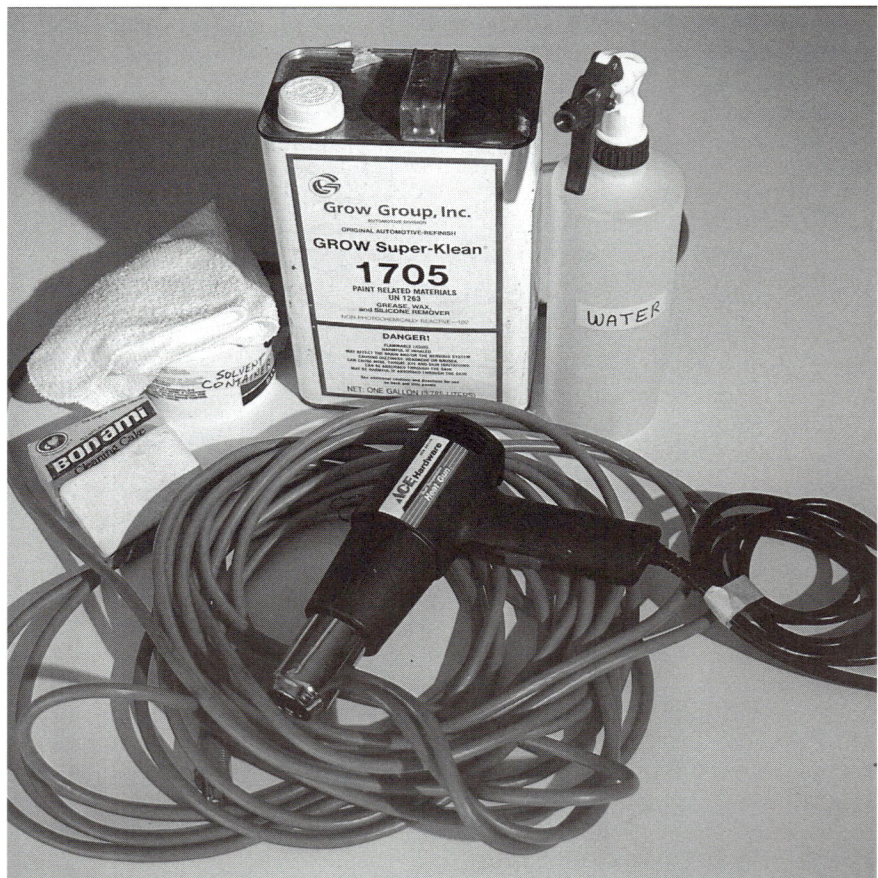

Preparation tools.

GridView.

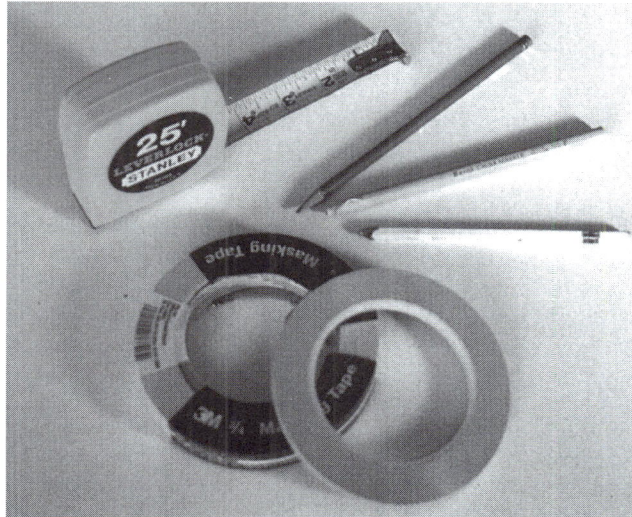
Layout tools.

performance calendered vinyl is acceptable as long as no Condition 1's are present.

Condition 3: 24-hour visibility. *Select:* Retro-reflective film products.

Condition 4: Easy removability. *Select:* Repositionable film products. Note: All films are repositionable and removable to the trained installer. Repositionable film's chief advantage is easier removability two or three years after installation.

Condition 5: Very short-term usage, easy removal, paint stencil. *Select:* calendered spray-mask vinyl film.

Condition 6: Backlit, high-visibility color. *Select:* High-performance cast translucent vinyl.

Condition 7: Very long-term expectations, resists solvents and graffiti, and holds up under high-UV exposure. *Select:* Ultra-high performance cast fluoropolymer film products.

ENVIRONMENTAL CONTROL

Master Principle: All environmental extremes are controlled by you.

Vinyl graphics enable an installer to exercise greater control over the environment than inks, paint, gilding, etc. The ideal temperature range for installing pressure-sensitive or self-adhesive vinyl films is from 40-90°F (4-32°C). Under hot conditions, water is used to rapidly draw heat from the application surface. The application can be accomplished before the surface has a chance to reheat.

Shade is your friend on a hot day; the sun is your ally on a cold day. Static conditions can be controlled by using anti-static dryer sheets, a light misting of water, rubbing alcohol or application fluids.

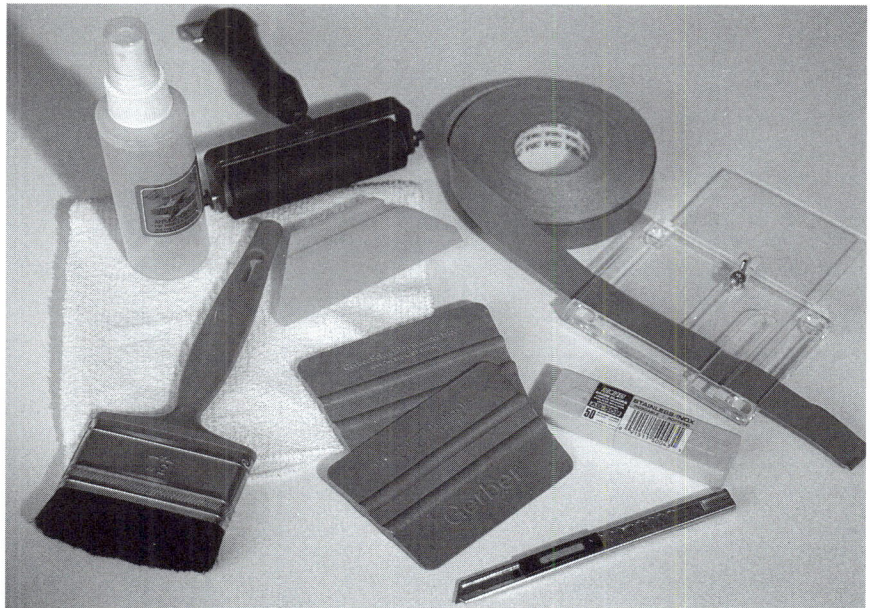
Application tools.

Removal tools.

MASK APPLICATION

Master Principle: Problems with the application tape or pre-mask will transfer problems to the finished vinyl application.

Application tape is used for transferring graphics from the release liner to the application surface. Three common problems encountered when placing the mask over the vinyl are: distortion, wrinkling and overlapping the mask.

These problems will exhibit themselves in the finished vinyl application by creating bubbles, wrinkles and misalignments. Avoid these problems by using mask of sufficient width to completely cover the full height of the graphics, by using a mask dispenser or applicator that will give you control over the mask application, and by using proper squeegee methods when applying the mask. Mask dispensers *(see photo at top right)* hold the mask taut and straight as it is pulled from the roll. A mask applicator *(see photo at middle right)* goes one step further and applies the mask in a relaxed distortion-free manner.

The proper way to squeegee the mask is to first pass over the center of the graphic and then use short, overlapping strokes to the edges *(see photo at bottom)*. Stroke firmly but avoid pushing or bunching the mask.

SUBSTRATE PREPARATION

Master Principle: Thorough preparation is the key to successful and long-lasting results.

Preparation of a surface prior to applying vinyl is essential. Fortunately, it is a simple process that requires only a few minutes and the use of effective, yet inexpensive chemicals.

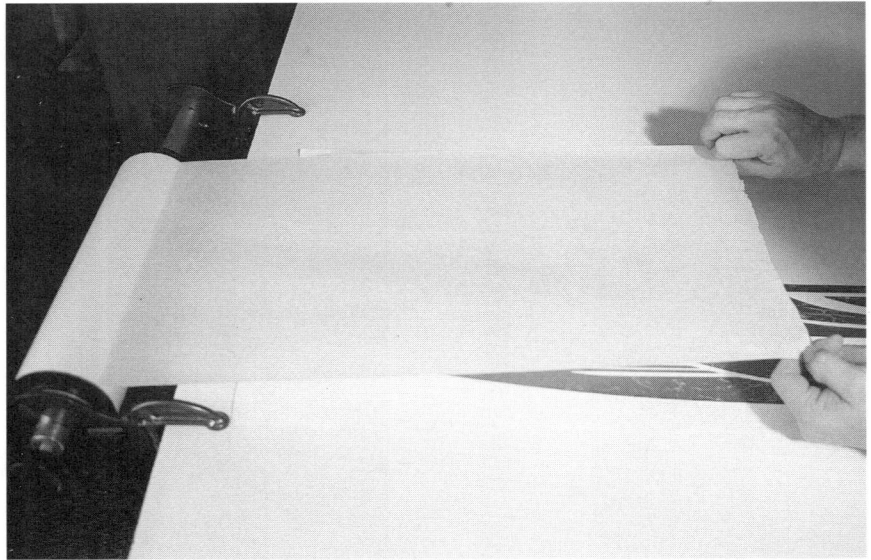

Mask dispensers hold the mask taut and straight.

Mask applicators free the mask of distortion.

Squeegee the mask in the center first, then use short overlapping strokes to the edges.

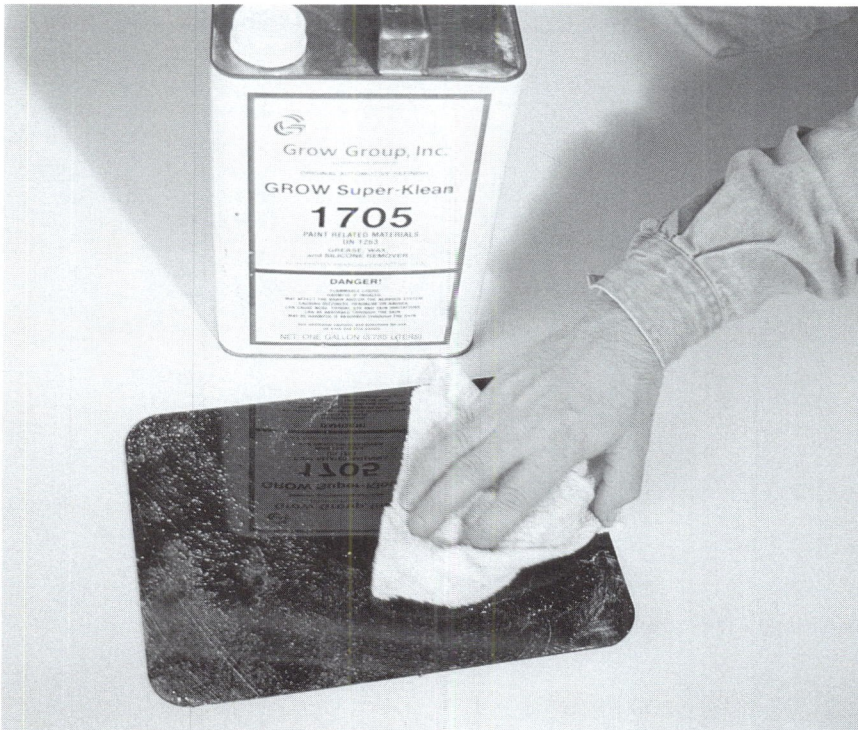

Use a second, clean towel to rub off the remover.

Two kinds of surface contamination have to be removed: petrochemical (tar, wax, grease, oil and gas residues, smoke films and polymer finishes); and organic (bug splatters, bird droppings, tree sap and common dust and dirt).

Petrochemical contaminants are quickly, safely and easily removed with automotive tar, wax and grease removers, which can be readily found at automotive paint supply stores. (Products that I have found effective are NAPA's Kleanz-Easy, Sherwin Williams' Sher-Will-Clean, and Ditzer's Wax and Grease Remover.) These products contain a combination of chemicals. A single solvent such as alcohol, denatured or isopropyl, is not 100% effective at removing the wide variety of possible contaminants. Stronger solvents, like reducers, thinners, acetone, etc., can damage the substrate material and often create an aggressive tooth that affects the repositionability of the vinyl adhesive. (Prep Sol is often recommended by vinyl manufacturers. It works, but I have found it

to be oilier and harder to remove than competitive products that work faster and just as effectively.)

Organic-contamination removal requires water. Common dishwater soap can be added sparingly to make the water "wetter." In a pinch, spit works fine, too.

There are some instances where exotic removers may be needed. For instance, boats with fiberglass hulls may have leftover mold-release agents present. A reducer, such as DuPont 3812S, will remove this contamination. Just watch for the tooth effect this may give the surface. While this may be desirable for hand-gilding gold, it can cause loss of repositionability for a pressure-sensitive film product.

Exotic removers may also be needed when a surface has been exposed to acid rain. This has been a common problem on many new vehicles in recent years. The fall-out left on the surface may have to be removed using a compound called Acidox and a buffing machine. The clearcoat finishes on modern vehicles sometimes resist the initial grip of the vinyl adhesive following prep with the wax and grease remover. In this case, keep a bar of Bon Ami (a soap with a mild abrasive) around. Wash over the application area with a paste from the Bon Ami using water and a clean towel. This will generally improve the initial "tackability."

Procedure is simple. With one towel, apply the tar, wax and grease remover. Use another clean towel to rub off the remover and any haze or film until the surface is clear (see photo at top left). If existing organic contaminants were not affected by the remover, then go back over the surface with water. If the surface was very dirty or dusty to begin with, you should go over the surface with plenty of water and then use the tar, wax and grease remover. Be as thorough as possible when cleaning any surface. The few extra seconds needed will save unnecessary problems.

LAYOUT AND POSITION
Master Principle: Use the correct guidelines, then measure twice and apply once. Good layout begins with recognition of proper layout principles that can be learned from such books as Mastering Layout *by Mike Stevens (available through ST Publications).*

Another guiding principle is to correctly measure centers, margins and reference points. Most applications are made on a horizontal axis, whether this be the edge of the substrate, window frame, or, in the case of a vehicle, a dominant horizontal axis that is parallel to the rocker panel

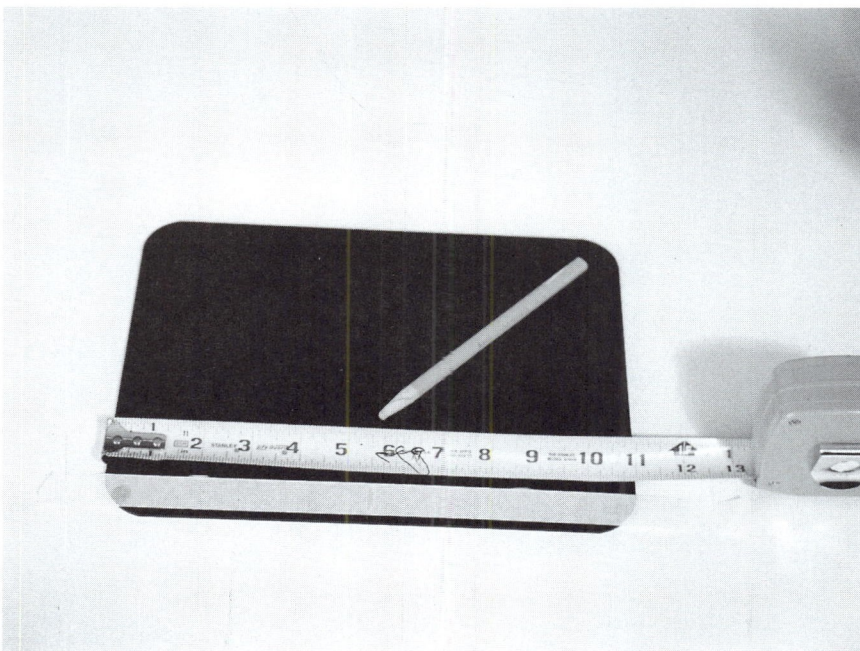

Mark two reference points between which tape can be tautly applied.

of the vehicle. Watch out for ascending or descending lines or body panels that have a pronounced convex contour. A masking tape line can serve as a quick position check before proceeding with the application.

After determining the correct position on the substrate, use a Stabilo pencil to mark two reference points between which a masking tape line can be tautly applied *(see photo on page 9)*. This tape guide can be marked for additional placement guidance for left, right or center justification and used repeatedly if handled carefully.

The hinge method is commonly used to suspend the graphic above the desired area prior to the actual application *(see photos on this page)*. This can be accomplished with a separate piece of 3/4-in. masking tape.

A faster, simpler method is to use the pre-mask itself as the hinge by rubbing the mask along the top edge after the release liner has been removed, or, in the case of a larger graphic, by rubbing a vertical line through the pre-mask between two elements of the graphic, and then squeegeeing just the first part of the

The hinge method suspends the graphic over the desired area.

graphic, followed by squeegeeing remaining portions of the graphic into position.

The main principle to remember, when using the hinge method, is to be certain you align the graphic from the starting position correctly along the axis you are following. The starting position can be from either the end, the center or anywhere along the graphic, as long as your have properly centered or justified the application.

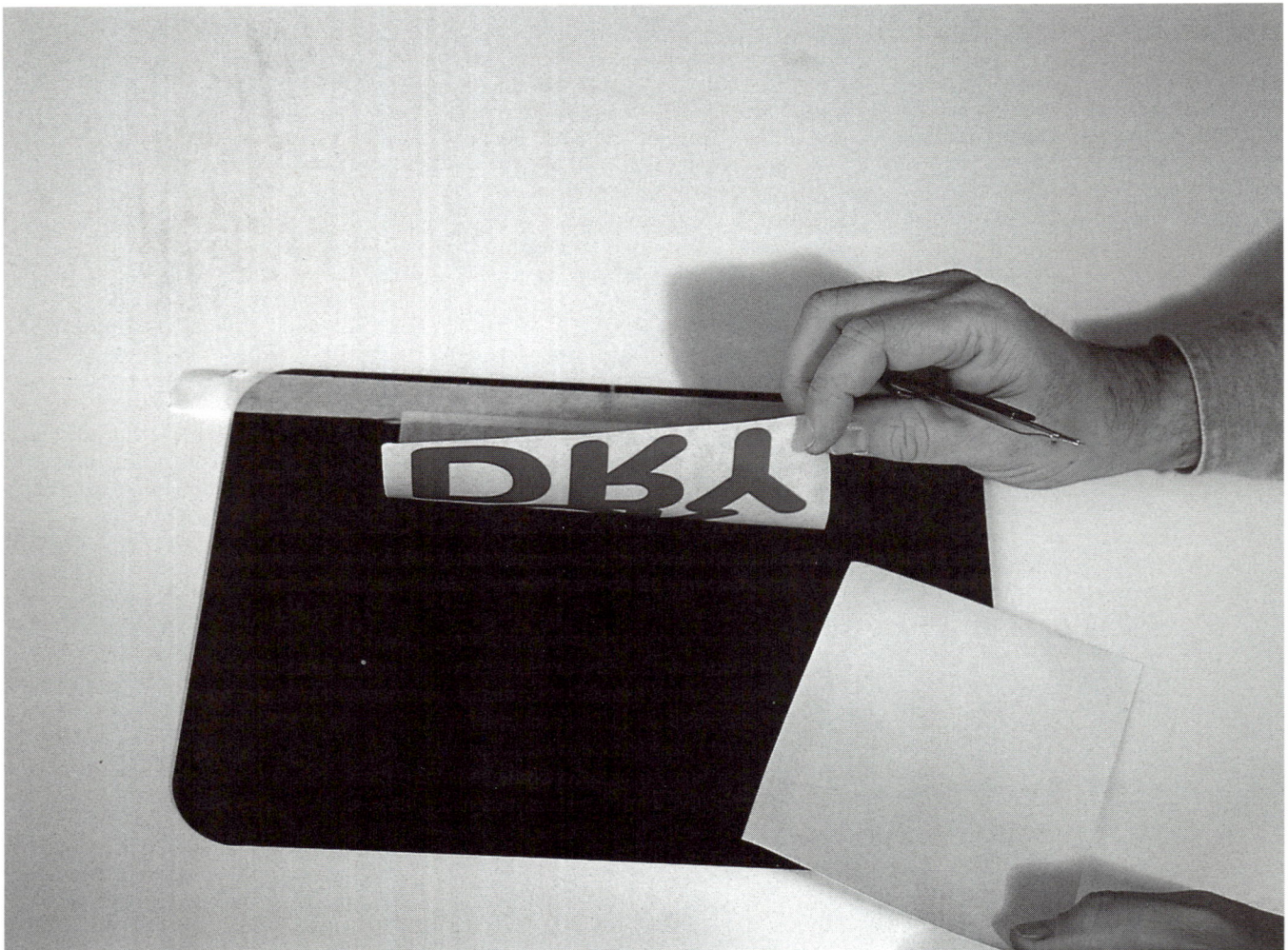

A separate piece of 3/4-in. masking tape acts as the hinge for accurate graphic placement.

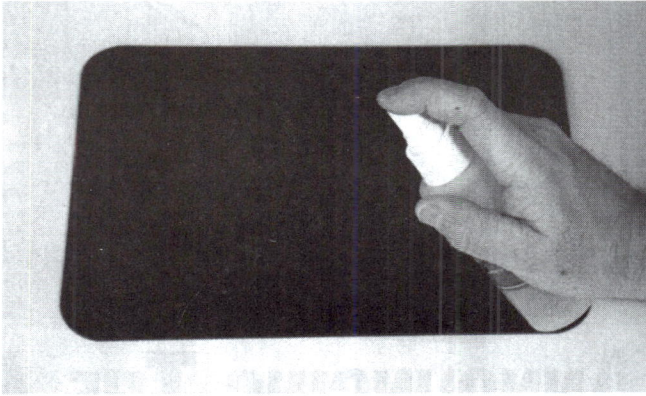

1) Spray the substrate.

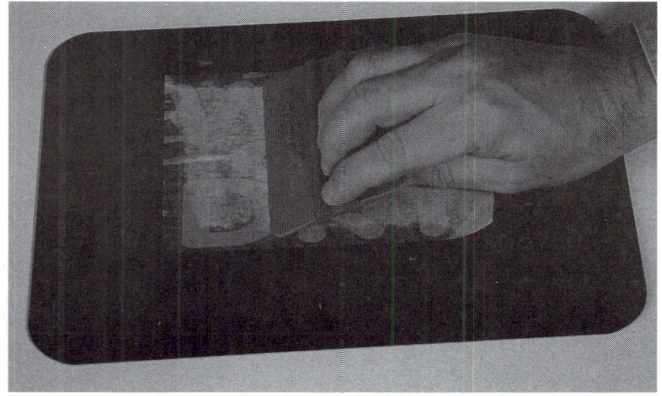

2) Remove the release liner from the graphic and spray the adhesive side.

3) Position the graphic where you want it.

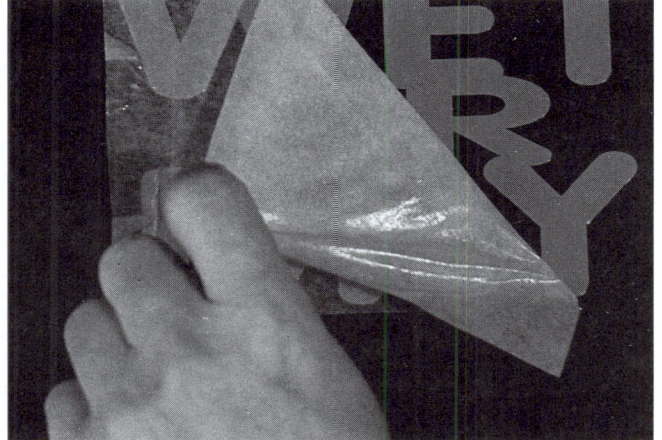

4) Squeegee properly.

5) Spray the mask. Allow the penetrating action of the solution to soften the latex (30-90 seconds depending on humidity).

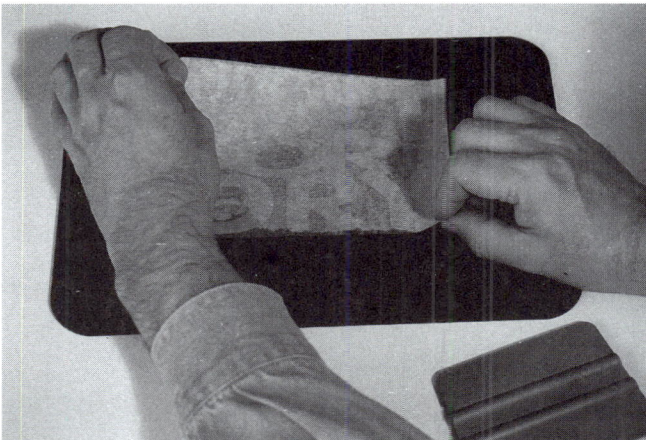

6) Re-squeegee and spray the mask again. Allow 15-30 seconds before carefully pulling the mask from the graphic.

WET AND DRY TECHNIQUES

Master Principle: Practice proper squeegee techniques so you can rely most often on dry application; wet application is your back-up.

At times, wet application may be preferred even by the experienced installer (with certain environmental conditions). Examples include when the surface is very hot or the substrate has a lot of static build-up, as is often the case with plastic surfaces. Other conditions favoring wet application are: very windy, when alignment is critical, transparent or translucent vinyls are being used, the graphic is too large to easily handle alone, the vinyl is unmasked or the installer is a novice. Wet applications will go much faster and easier if a professional application solution is used instead of soap and water.

Experienced installers usually prefer dry application when conditions are favorable. Dry is definitely preferred with small letters or components, with striping and on compound curves or textured substrates.

Applying the Film

PROPER SQUEEGEE USE

Master Principle: Work from the center out with short, overlapping strokes to the edges.

Squeegee: Anything an installer uses to properly apply a graphic to a substrate. Your finger or the side of your hand can be used as a squeegee for small graphics or 2-in.-wide striping. Squeegees may be made from plastic, nylon or rubber. A wide, stainless-steel blade also can be used to squeegee application tape to vinyl graphics. One very special squeegee is the surface-conforming squeegee, often referred to as a rivet brush.

By far, the most common squeegee is a simple single- or double-bladed piece of stiff plastic that is usually 4 in. wide and comes in a variety of colors. This type of squeegee is typically used for applying graphics on flat substrates. If the blade is not rigid enough, or is worn or nicked, as is typical with "bondo" spreader-type squeegees, the application will often suffer from bubbles and/or wrinkles.

A nylon squeegee (typically gold-colored) is preferred for applying vinyl graphics to flat substrates because it does not wear out on the edge the way plastic ones do. If you have been using a squeegee for applying paper mask, you will notice a lot of edge wear, and it is best not to use that same squeegee for applying vinyl.

Unmasked, raw vinyl can be applied by using wet application and a rubber squeegee that slips readily on wet surfaces *(see photo above right)*.

The surface-conforming squeegee *(see photo at right)* is simply an inexpensive nylon paint brush that has had the bristles cut down to approximately 3/4-in. in length. The bristle pattern should be fairly dense. This squeegee will press vinyl down into a textured surface or around the head of a rivet because it conforms to the contours of the substrate. More expensive rivet brushes are available, but these brushes tend to have the following dynamics: the bristle pattern is usually less dense; the bristles are larger in diameter (which are harsher to the vinyl); and they don't conform as well to textured substrates.

Unmasked vinyl can be applied using wet application techniques.

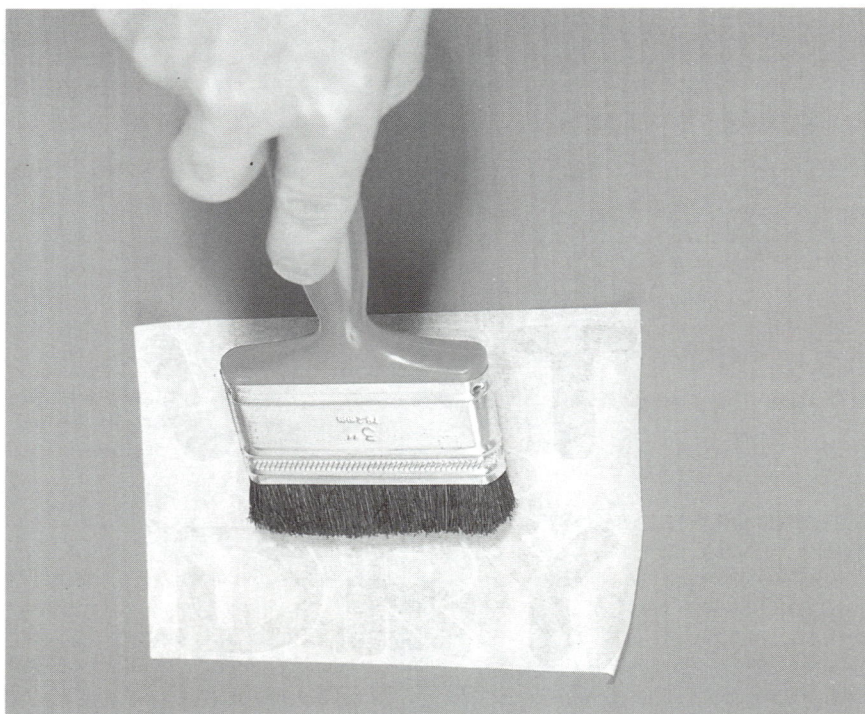

Specialized tools, such as this trimmed nylon brush, are needed for conforming vinyl to irregular surfaces.

Rubber rollers or brayers are useful for applying vinyl graphics, but the point of contact is broader, which produces less pressure than a stiff plastic squeegee.

Rubber rollers or brayers are often used for mask and graphic application *(see photo above)*. When used correctly, these tools work well. However, the point of contact is generally broader than the edge of a squeegee, and consequently, it may be necessary to go back over a rolled application with a stiff squeegee to increase the downforce for a tighter tack to the surface. In addition, rollers also have metal parts than can accidentally damage the graphic or substrate.

The main difference between an experienced installer and a novice is generally the amount of time they've spent using a squeegee properly.

Whether wet or dry application is done, it is essential to use the squeegee correctly. Place the squeegee roughly 45° from the surface *(see photo at right)* and use moderate pressure. Squeegee the center of the graphic first, then use short, overlapping strokes and work toward the edges. Keep the vinyl from making

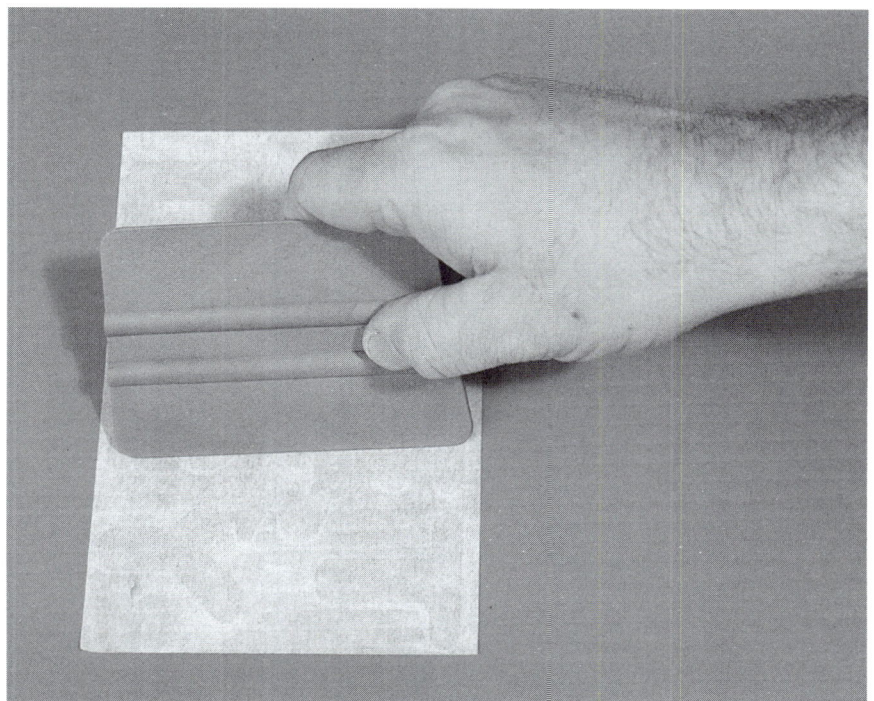

Squeegees should be applied at a 45° angle to the surface.

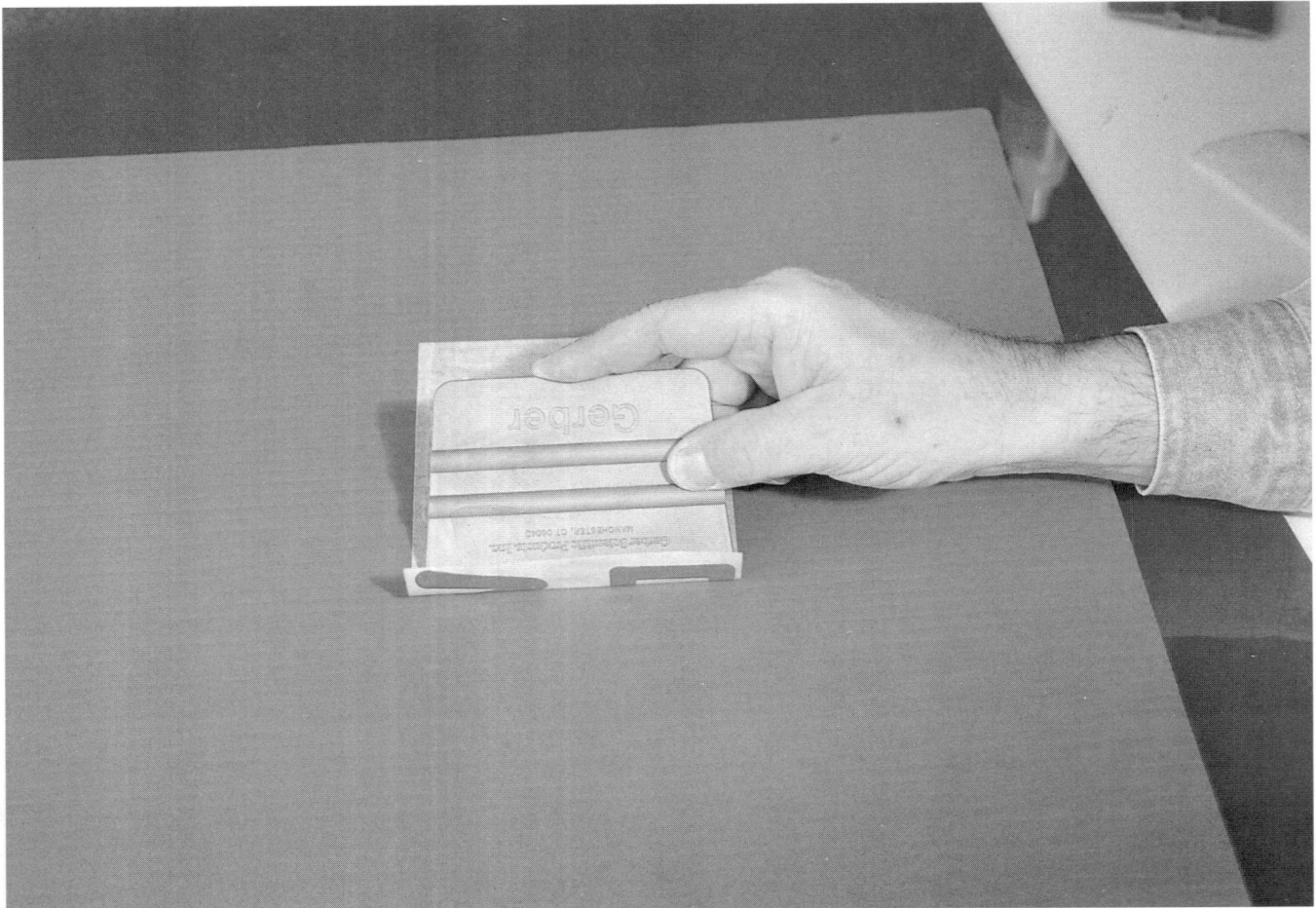

Squeegee the center of the graphic first, then use short, overlapping strokes and work toward the edges.

contact with the application surface; let the squeegee do the work *(see photo above)*. Repeat these actions with a slightly firmer pressure (it takes only seconds). Prior to removing the mask, use a finger to firmly burnish the edges of the graphic components. After the mask is removed, use a towel over your hand to reburnish the entire graphic *(see photo at right)*. A friction sleeve over your squeegee can also be used to prevent scratches on unmasked vinyl. Or, you can lightly spray the vinyl and stroke the graphics with an uncovered squeegee. To summarize: use the squeegee correctly; let the squeegee do the work of placing the vinyl in contact with the surface; and avoid scratching the vinyl.

SQUEEGEE MAINTENANCE
Master Principle: The best applications are done with the right squeegee that is properly cared for.

A squeegee with a bad edge is worthless. Do *not* mix up your mask-application squeegees with the ones you use for vinyl application. When the edge deteriorates, sharpen or re-place it. A typical plastic squeegee can be resharpened by running the edge along the grip channel on another squeegee. But once the edge gets too worn or nicked, replace it.

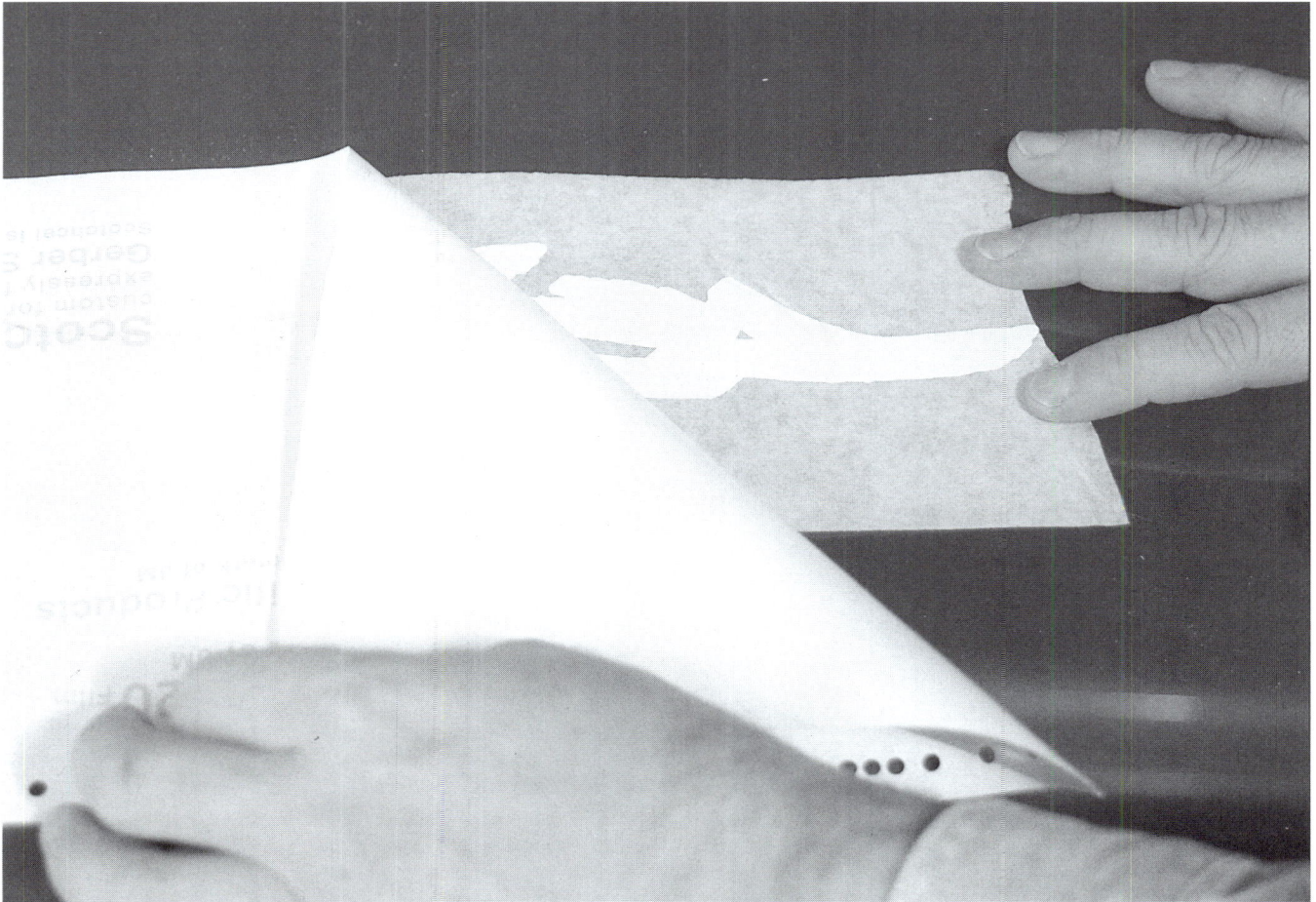

Pull the release liner away from the adhesive side of the vinyl at a 180° angle, folding the liner back on itself. This helps transfer the graphic to the pre-mask correctly.

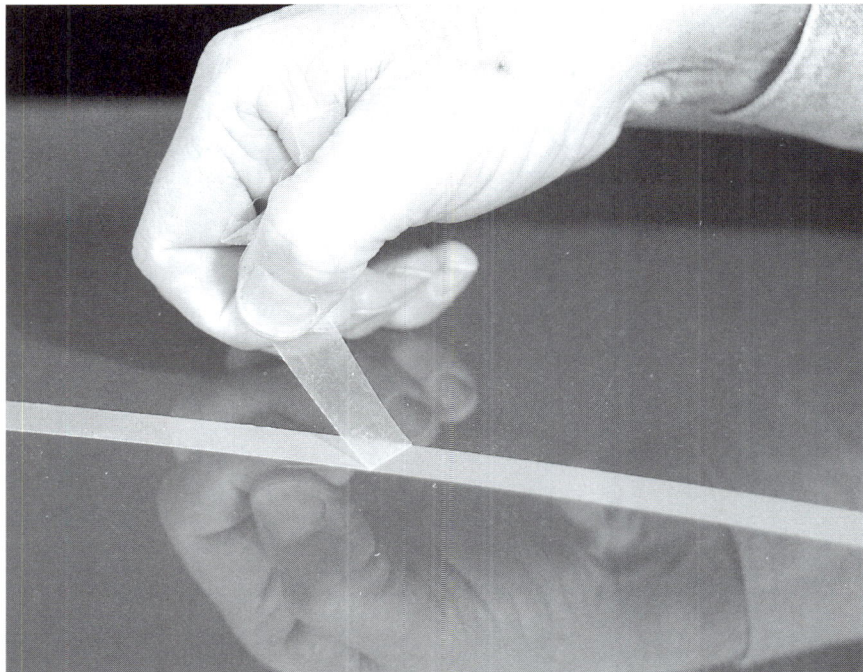

Clear mask on vinyl striping helps it flex and turn.

REMOVING THE RELEASE LINER

Master Principle: Remove the liner instead of lifting the graphic.

It is important to keep the graphic tight to the pre-mask until it has been firmly tacked to the application surface. If you try to lift the graphic with the mask, you may loosen the mask's grip on the graphic. A foolproof way to correctly remove the liner instead of the graphic is to lay the graphic face down on a flat surface with the pre-mask on the surface. Then, roll the release liner away from the adhesive side of the graphic, back over itself at 180° (*see photo above*).

Calendered films have a matte or semi-matte surface that may adhere better to a high-tack mask. Textured film products will require a mask with a very high tack, which is available from some sign-supply distributors. Mask applied to textured films should be re-burnished *prior* to application because the mask has a tendency to loosen its grip if left in place for more than a few minutes.

Masks on smooth films tend to tighten their grip over time. Paper masks will generally have a higher tack than clear polyethylene masks. Striping can have either paper or polyethylene masks. The clear plastic masks on striping allow flexing and

Friction sleeves can be purchased to cover and protect the edge of the standard 4-in. squeegee. You can make your own from recycled Tyvek® envelopes or floppy-disk sleeves. Teflon plumber's tape, a towel or application tape also can be wrapped on the edge to help preserve it and provide slip.

Use the right squeegee for the right job. Textured substrates and compound surfaces require surface-conforming squeegees. When working with a heat gun or on hot surfaces, avoid melting your squeegee.

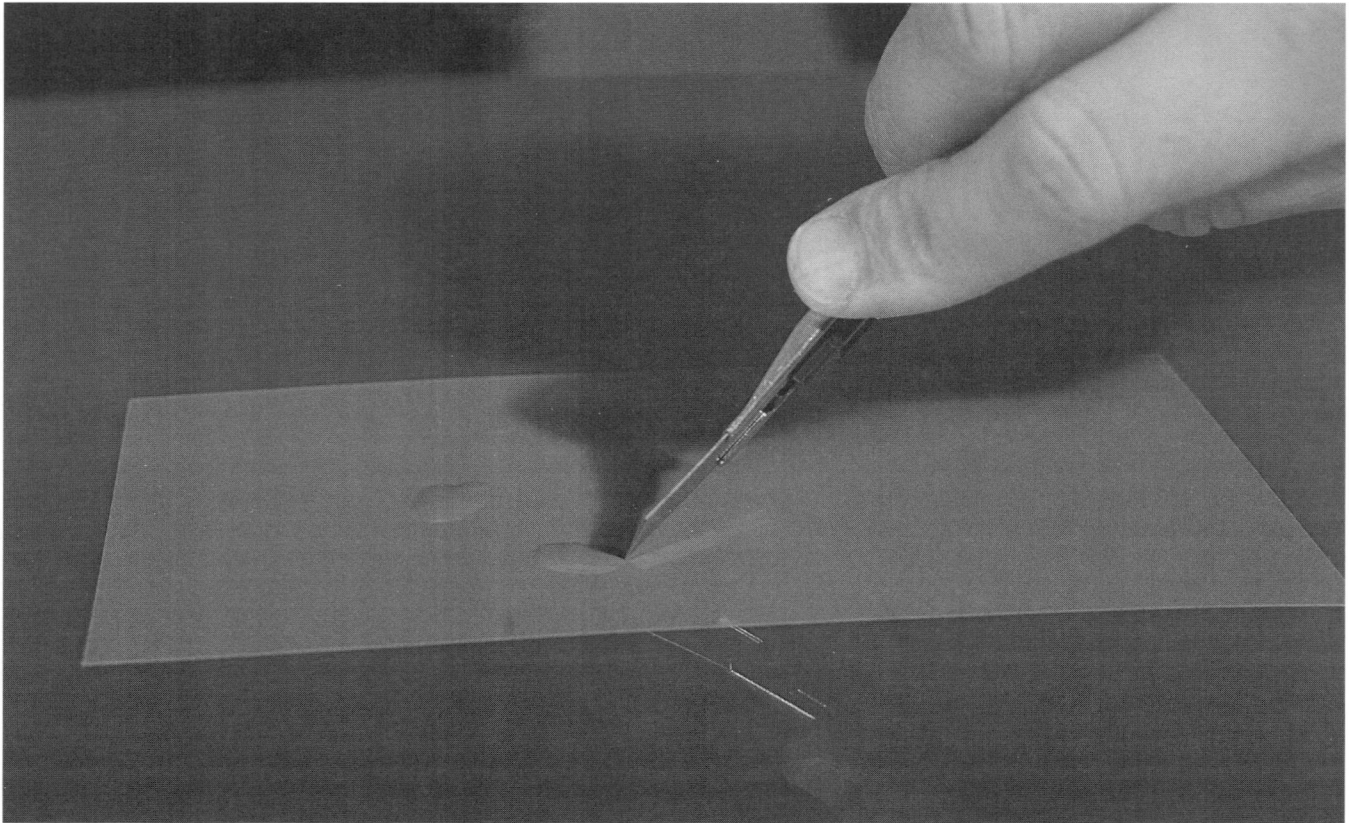

To remove bubbles in a graphic, pierce the film at the bubble's edge (above) and then force the air or water out of the opening with your finger or squeegee (below).

turning. The clear mask must always be removed after application *(see photo on page 15)*. Leaving it on, especially on outdoor applications, will eventually ruin the stripe.

Store vinyl graphics away from heat and humidity. Do not get the release liner wet. Moisture will go through the paper and break down the silicone release layer in the liner, causing it to stick to the adhesive side of the graphic. Should this occur, use application fluid on any liner material that sticks to the adhesive and lift the bits of wet liner using the blade of a knife.

REMOVING APPLICATION TAPE
Master Principle: Pull application tape 180° back over itself, then re-squeegee.

The climactic conclusion occurs when you remove the application tape from the installed graphic. If you have done everything properly to this stage, the graphic should be tightly adhered to the substrate and should be smooth without bubbles or wrinkles. Don't rush. Watch for loose edges and reburnish before proceeding with the pull.

If bubbles are present, simply puncture them at the bottom edge with the point of a knife or a pin *(see photo at the top of the page)*. Then, push the air or fluid out of the hole with your finger *(see photo at right)* or squeegee. Very small acne-like bubbles will generally disappear by themselves within a few days as the graphic goes

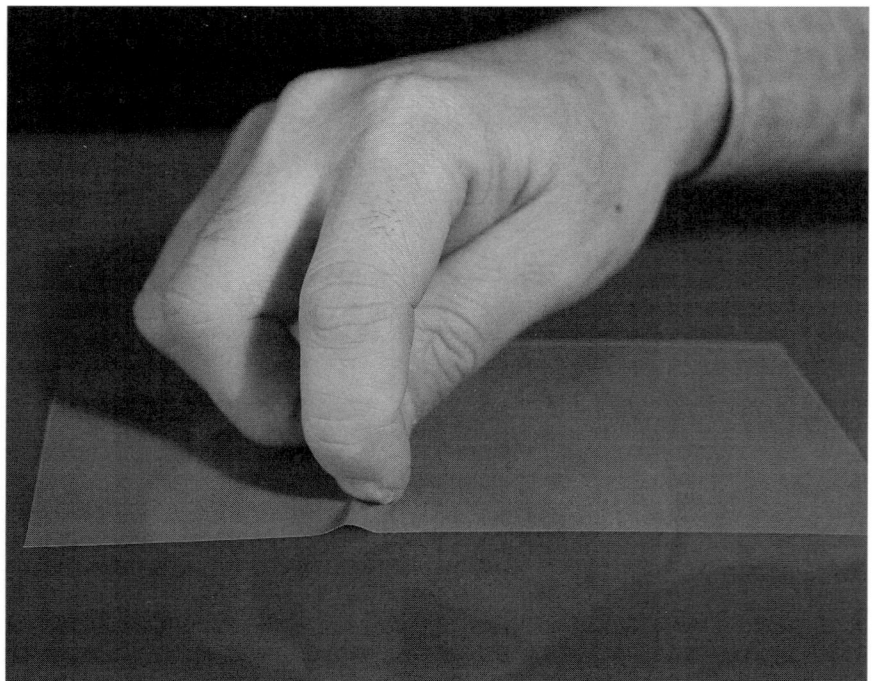

through a few temperature cycles. Tiny bubbles will contract and make contact with the surface and not rise again. Just be sure to pop the big ones, or the adhesive will dry out, and the vinyl will crack in time.

Wrinkles should be prevented by following the recommended application procedures. If, however, you get a small wrinkle, you may be able to remove it by

pressing from the interior end of the wrinkle out toward the edge of the graphic with the back of your fingernail *(see top photo on page 17)*. This action helps spread or redistribute and flatten the wrinkles. The only remedy for a severe wrinkle is to either re-do the graphic or carefully slice with your knife along the wrinkle and overlap the edges. The overlap is preferable to a raised, air-holding ridge of vinyl *(see bottom photo)*.

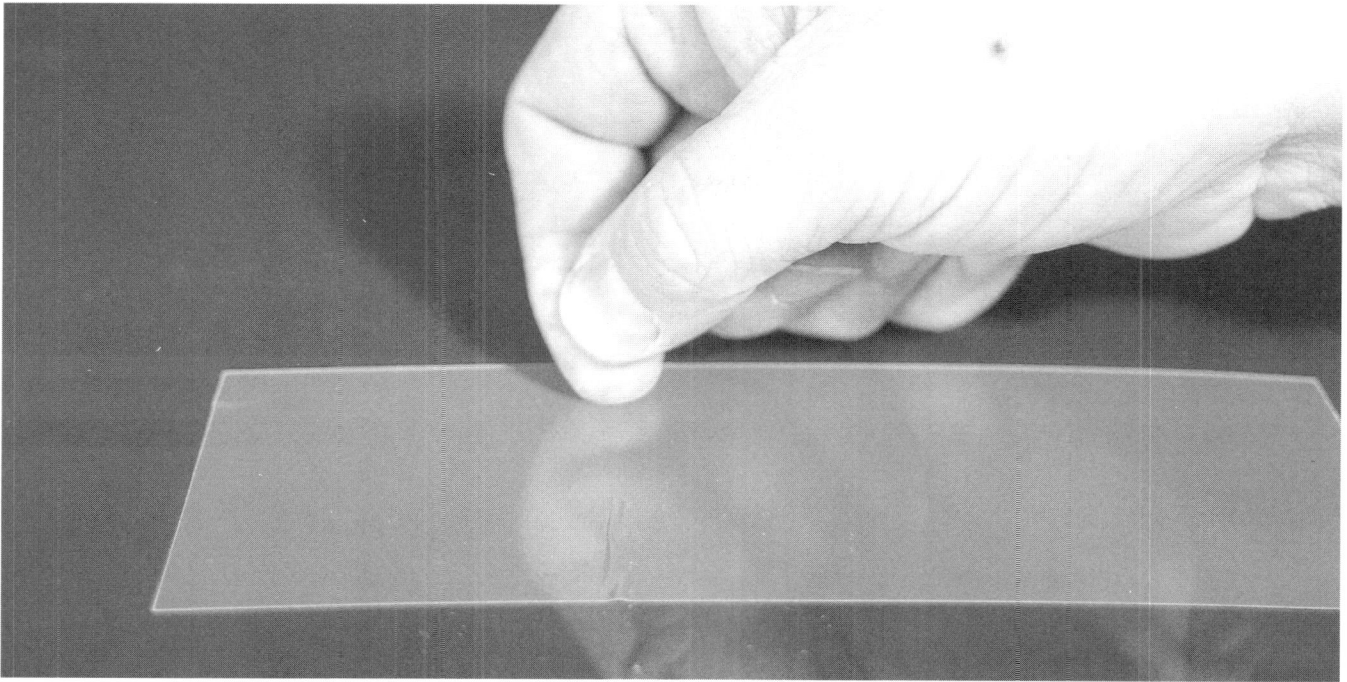

You can remove small wrinkles with your fingernail by pushing toward the edge to redistribute excess material.

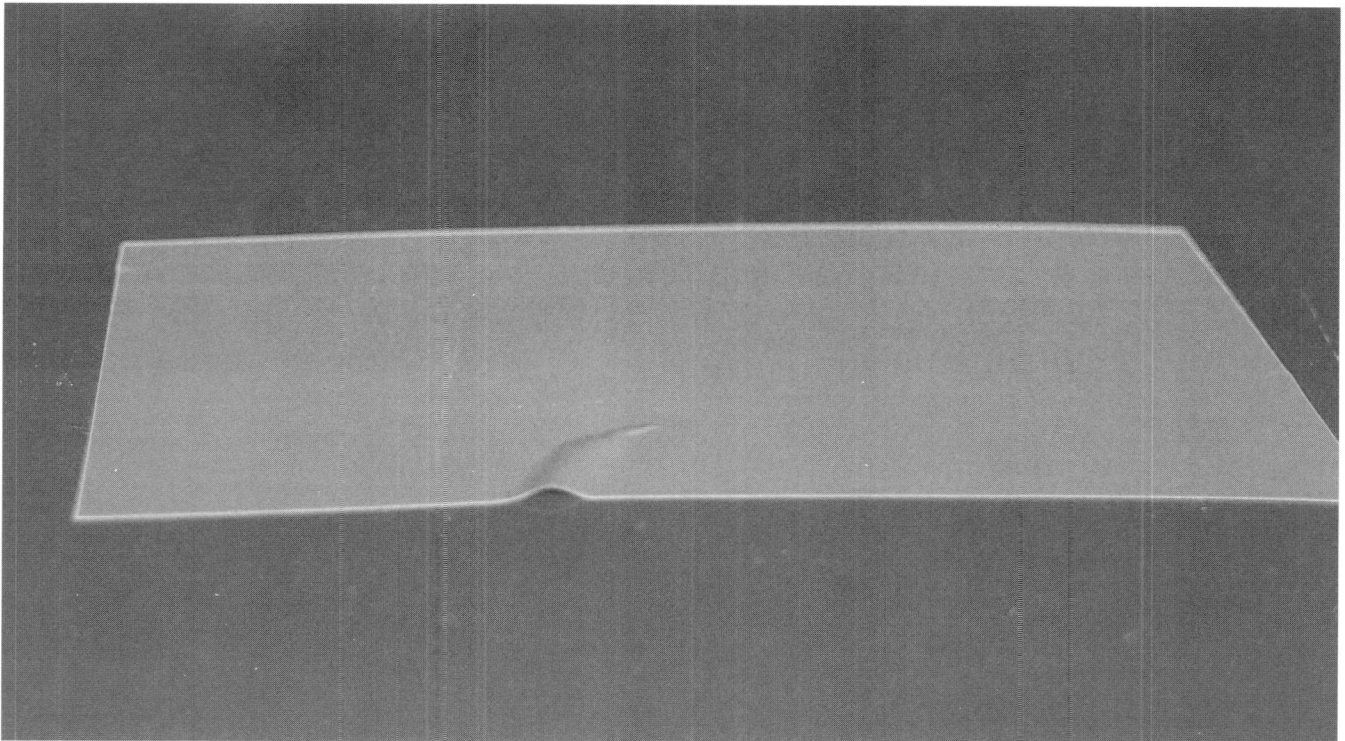

Severe wrinkles should be slit to overlap material if they can't be redistributed. This is preferred to leaving an air pocket in the vinyl.

Do a final, quick inspection of your application. Give special attention to edges, tips and points; be sure they are tacked down. Clean the surrounding area of the substrate to remove smudges, fluid run-off, etc. Take photos and measurement notes in case you need to duplicate the installation in the future. Sign your work if you are proud of it and want the job to advertise for repeat and referral work.

PRICING

Master Principle: Be sure to charge for your work in proportion to the value your client has received.

The value of your work is not determined by the cost of your materials. It is determined by the value of the quality, service, creativity and perceived benefits you have given your client. Use a standardized system of pricing as outlined in the *Computer Vinyl Graphics Pricing Guide* (available through ST Publications) to bring the authority of the written word to your pricing routine.

Master Principle: Continued practicing of excellent fundamentals gives you the foundation for advanced performance and superior results.

Registration and Repair

VINYL APPLICATION often requires using advanced techniques to manage difficult application conditions or more visually creative designs. Such techniques are needed for:
1) multi-component registration,
2) damaged or contaminated graphics,
3) detailed graphics involving dimensional perspective and paint effects,
4) extreme temperatures,
5) compound curves and corrugated surfaces,
6) striping techniques when cutting, turning and tapering,
7) textured or porous substrates and
8) easy, rapid film removal.

MULTI-COMPONENT REGISTRATION

Master principle: Registering multiple components is simply coordinating hand and eye movement with a relaxed approach to surface contact on the substrate or prior layer of film.

Registration of multiple elements or colors of vinyl requires the careful coordination of your motions with surface contact. Premature contact may result in misalignment and ruined graphics. This need not occur if you first learn to relax with the materials. You should understand that contact does not necessarily mean bonding has taken place; you can release the film by quickly snapping the application away from the surface. The adhesive can make contact and still be repositioned, prior to any burnishing action. Possible exceptions might include smooth glass surfaces or plastic — situations in which wet application would be appropriate to avoid aggressive, initial attachment of the adhesive.

Wet application is commonly employed to help reposition graphics. However, a skilled applicator can use the aforementioned "snapping" motion to perform dry registration, thereby saving time and money. Generally, dry registration requires more hands-on practice with the film products until the installer is very comfortable handling and repositioning them.

Registration blocks or circles can also be used to align components or colors. This involves cutting small squares on each sheet in identical positions and placing them on top of one another. Although this procedure

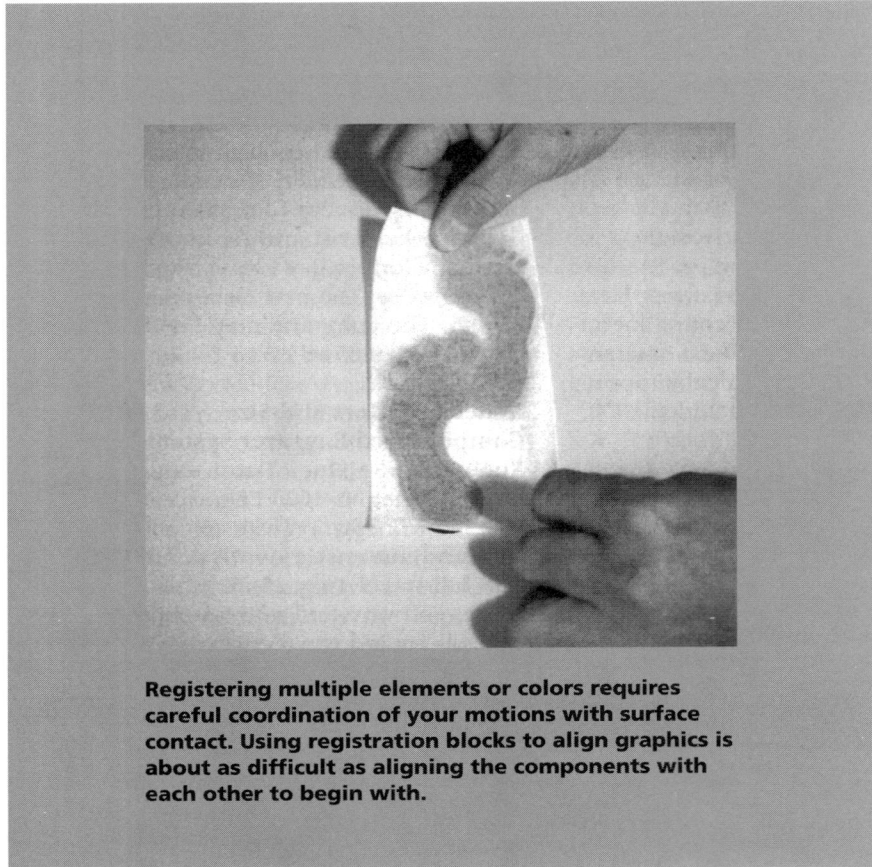

Registering multiple elements or colors requires careful coordination of your motions with surface contact. Using registration blocks to align graphics is about as difficult as aligning the components with each other to begin with.

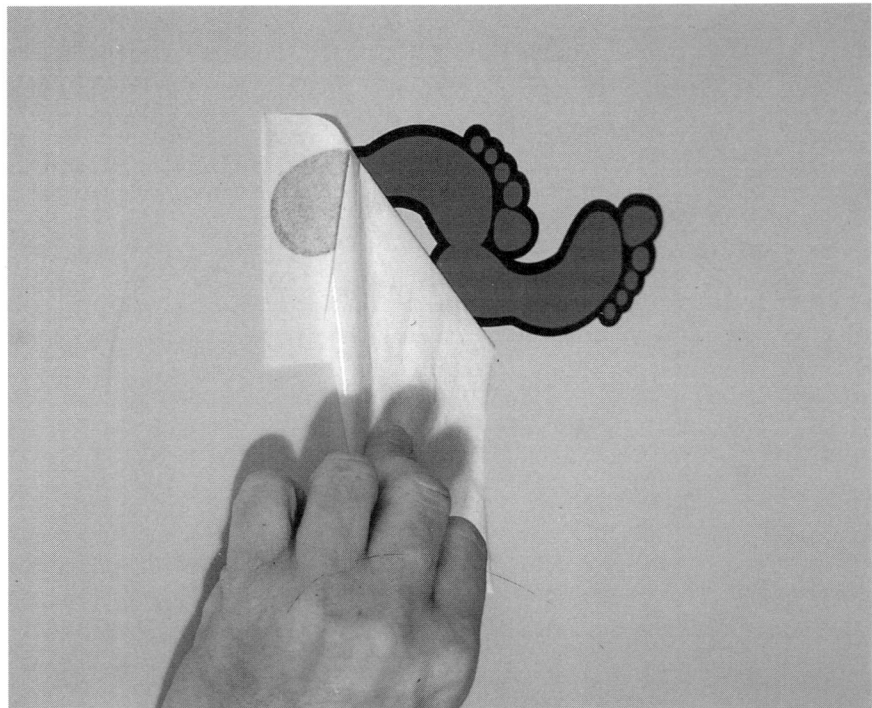

Attaining good, consistent registration requires practice and mastery of the basic application principles outlined in the previous chapter.

works, I rarely use it because of the time required to generate the registration shapes. Alignment of these shapes atop one another is as difficult as simply aligning the components with each other in the first place.

If necessary, I note or draw a portion of the graphics to illustrate proper spacing of the various components. But usually there is just one way for them to fit together, much like a jigsaw puzzle.

Work with only a portion of the "puzzle" at a time, aligning only the amount of graphic you can easily handle between two hands (about 12-18 in.). On larger or longer graphics, only roll back the 12-18 in. of release liner you are working to align. Once you've correctly positioned your first foot-long segment, the balance of the graphic should easily align section-by-section — providing you don't stretch or distort the graphic. (This is another skill you will want to practice until you have learned to relax with the film.) Note: be sure to stack colors in the proper order or sequence so the finished picture is correct.

Application tape or mask can affect your ability to position graphics. Although clear application tapes are easy-to-use, they may require a friction sleeve on your squeegee. In addition, they may impede the easy removal of the mask when wet application is necessary. Because they're translucent, paper masks can be easily seen through when the application comes in close proximity to the surface; this is particularly true during wet applications. Again, the close proximity required for this work means the installer must be relaxed and aware that surface-contact does not necessarily mean bonding.

Multi-component registration can be accomplished with a SpeedPress™ too. Because this simple device is most easily used at a tabletop, it's generally found in shops. However, it is also usable outside the shop when graphics are being applied to a flat substrate. Using the tool may require two installers: one to hold the SpeedPress and another to do the application. Thin felt and/or magnetic strips adhesively mounted to the SpeedPress's aluminum frame will keep the frame

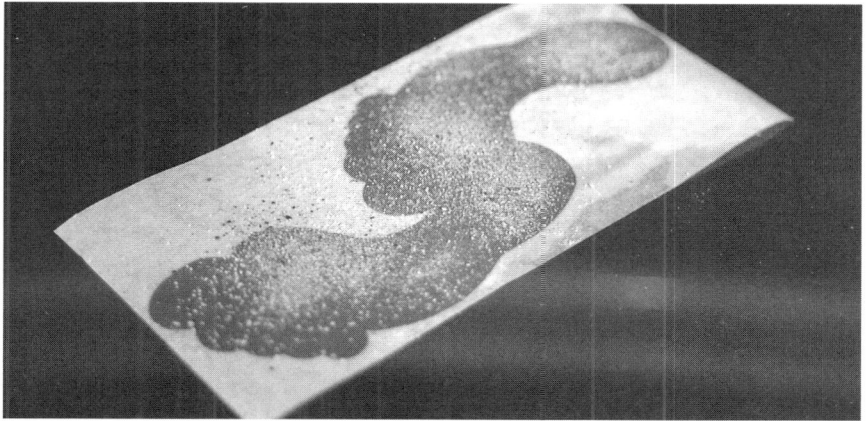

When a graphic gets dropped in the dirt (*above*), don't throw it away. Graphics are very forgiving in the hands of the trained installer, and there are several simple methods that can be used to undo, camouflage or repair damaged graphics.

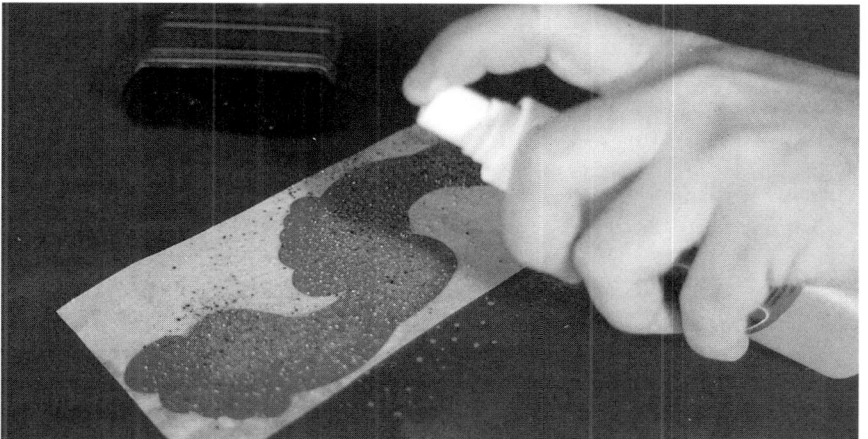

Application fluid can be sprayed on the contaminated surface . . .

. . . and then cleaned with a nylon paint brush.

from marring or scratching the substrate and create a hands-free steel substrate attachment capability. Attachable suction cups added to the frame will hold it on smooth plastic faces or glass.

When using the SpeedPress, remember that a flat, smooth surface is needed to lift the film from the release liner. The SpeedPress holds a clear pressure-sensitive film and you should position it over *unmasked* vinyl. Then press the film down on the vinyl with a rubber roller. The film will grab the vinyl and the release liner can be pushed off contact with the vinyl. Reposition the SpeedPress over the application surface and look through the clear film carrier to achieve proper alignment. Subsequent components or colors can likewise be transferred and aligned for proper registration. Apply each by using the rubber roller to press the vinyl adhesive into contact with the surface. Thus, multi-component registration is achieved using no mask whatsoever. The transfer film product that comes with SpeedPress comes in two levels of adhesion and can be used several times before replacement. Use a more aggressive transfer film when applying calendered vinyls than when applying cast films because cast films have a smoother surface.

REPAIR AND RECOVERY METHODS
Master principle: A vinyl graphic that has been damaged or contaminated can often be saved rather than replaced.

Vinyl graphics are very forgiving in the hands of the trained installer. Should there be a blunder during your application, several methods can be used to eliminate the need to make all new graphics. These techniques can undo, camouflage, or repair damaged graphics. Even graphics that have been dropped in the dirt with the adhesive exposed can be saved.

If the vinyl sticks to itself when the release liner is removed, for example, it is often possible to remove the film by quickly snapping the vinyl loose. Practice with some scrap vinyl and you'll learn you can indeed separate vinyl that has made contact with its own adhesive system. This technique also works when one character folds

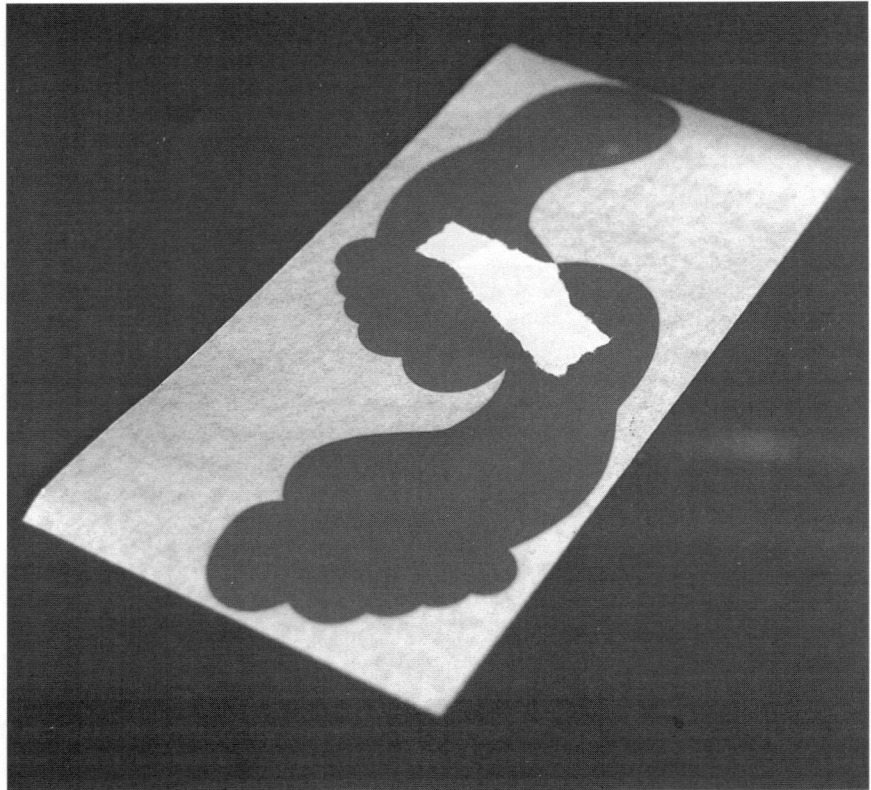

If a graphic is damaged by paper sticking to its adhesive, loosen the paper with application fluid . . .

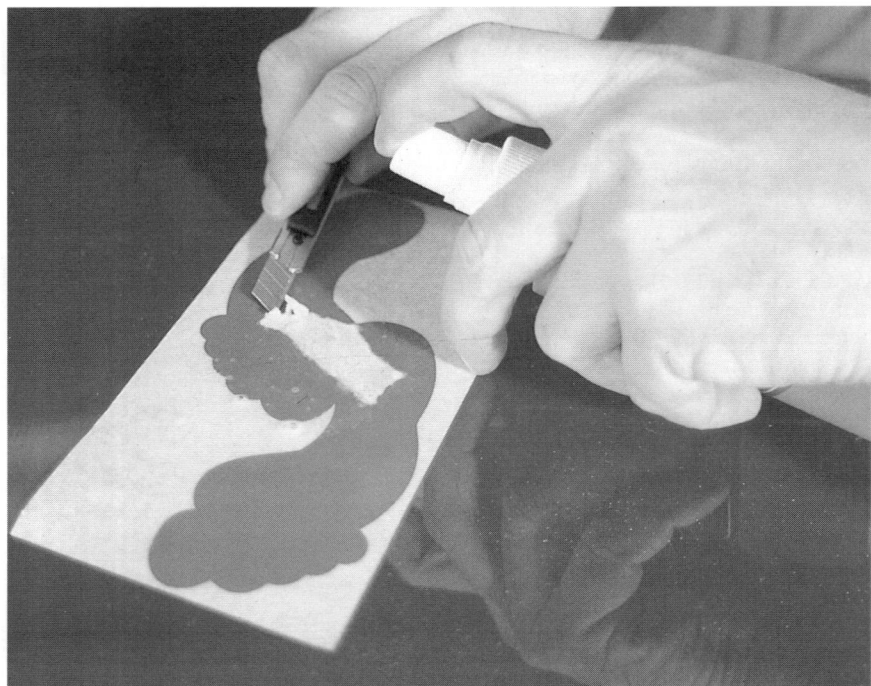

. . . then, pick up the paper with the point of your knife. Any additional small pieces can be brushed away.

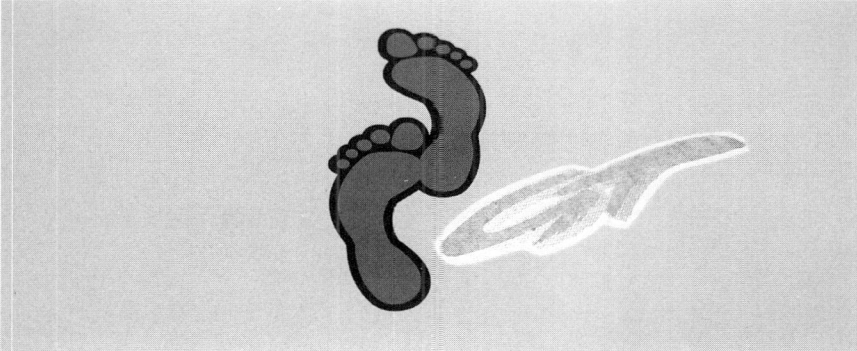

By understanding what viewers "see," you can blend paint and vinyl to create multi-dimensional effects.

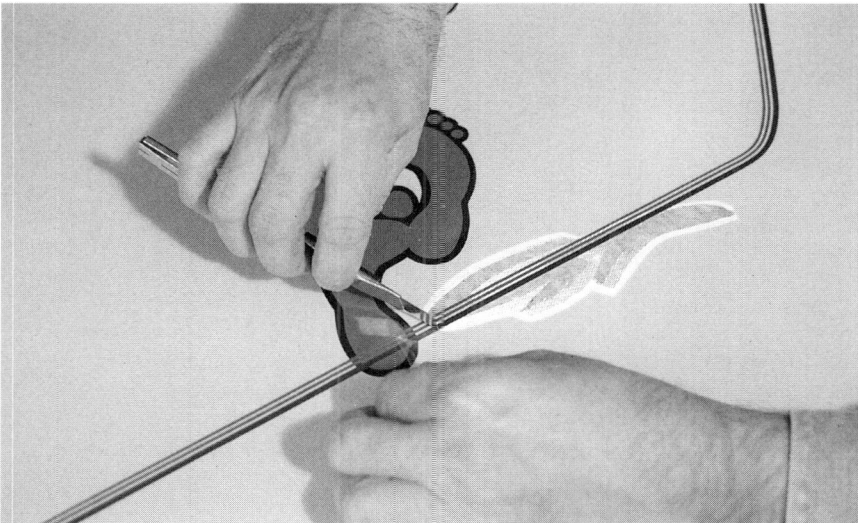

Notice how the vinyl stripe is laid over the feet graphic and the pre-masked "GT" graphic.

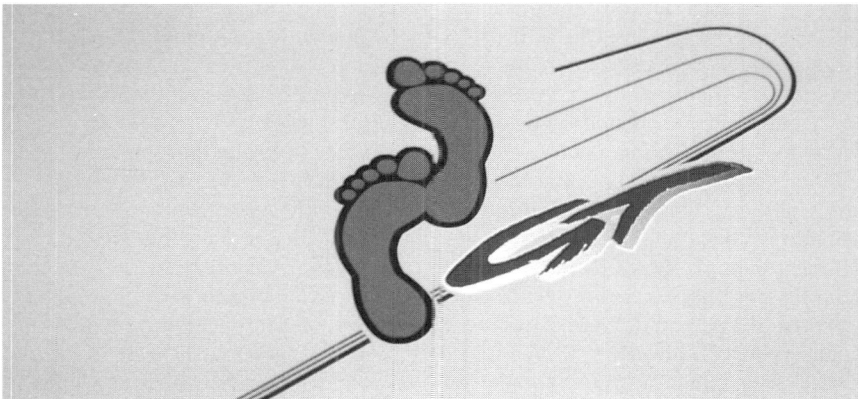

By cutting the strip around the graphics, it appears to withdraw into the background.

over on another. For extreme situations where the contact is particularly aggressive, application fluid may also help. Put a little of the application fluid in the juncture of the adhesive contact area and carefully snap small portions at a time, or pull gradually if the vinyl is not distorting. Moistening fingers that are in contact with the adhesive side will help them avoid sticking to and distorting the film.

An application that has been scraped or torn may be repaired by replacing the damaged area or the component. If you choose to replace the damaged area, make a clean, surgical cut that you can replace with a smooth-cut patch. It is handy to carry some scrap pieces of the same colors you'll be installing, should this type of repair become necessary. To lessen the profile, the edge of your knife can be used to gently rub the edge overlap. Applying heat will further facilitate hiding replacement pieces or mending tears; it makes patches more moldable and allows you to stretch the edges over and under each other.

Patching may be a perfectly acceptable option as well, especially if the graphics are being viewed from a distance. Otherwise, just replace the smallest single-piece component. Prior to removing a damaged section, use a piece of application tape over it for tracing paper. Transfer the tracing by smoothly applying it to a piece of raw vinyl and hand-cutting the new component. Then, apply this field-cut component to the affected area. So that you can place the newly cut piece correctly in position, it is often helpful to mark the location of the damaged component on the substrate with a marker or masking tape.

What do you do if the adhesive side of a graphic gets dropped in the dirt? Don't throw it away! Wash it! Application fluid can be sprayed on the contaminated adhesive. Simply use a clean nylon paint brush to brush the dirt and fluid off the side of the graphic. Then, blot the edge of the application tape with a towel. Blotting removes the dirty solution before it can soak into the masking and cause de-lamination. This method also works when vinyl contacts paper and sticks to it. The paper can be loosened with application fluid and picked up with the point of a knife. Small bits can be brushed off with a nylon brush or a moistened finger.

If you notice a particle of dirt or sand under an application, rub it with the back of your fingernail. Gentle massage will often make it pop-up through the vinyl; the hole you have created will then lie back down and effectively seal and disappear. If a bug gets trapped under the vinyl (it happens!), you may be able to carefully release the vinyl's closest edge and extract the creature. Otherwise, make a small, clean incision and remove the insect with the point of your knife.

DIMENSION AND PAINT EFFECTS
Master principle: Visual creativity and layouts are enhanced by thinking dimensionally to create illusions of depth and perspective. Blending the use of paint and vinyl quickly adds color, dimension and texture.

Using paint highlights and details on vinyl graphics can metamorphose the ordinary into the extraordinary. Highlights create texture, make colors visually realistic, and add body to an otherwise flat production. Learn from the creative artistry of painters by investing in some books on paint techniques and by following the work of skillful sign artists regularly featured in sign trade publications.

Outlining by itself increases contrast, but shadowing adds depth. Shadows make the primary graphic seem to project beyond the flat surface of the substrate. Skillfully applied, paint shadow techniques and newly developed shadow-effect films can make the primary graphic appear to float. Keep in mind that realistic shadows are made by darkening the color-value of the background, not by darkening the color value of the primary graphic. Depth illusion within a character itself

is created by adding angular lines for a convex effect, curvy lines for a balloon effect, or a combination or wavy lines and blended colors for a horizon effect. Surface area on the character is created by chrome effects which cause an illusion of reflected light from that surface.

Additional perspective is created by combining elements that underlie the primary graphic. These are elements that have been reduced in size so they appear to withdraw into the background. Consider how real objects have a foreground, middleground, and often multiple backgrounds. You can make your production appear multi-dimensional by visualizing how various graphic elements spatially relate to one another. Closer objects must take on larger relative size, while background elements must become progressively smaller so they appear to recede into the distance *(see photos on page 21).*

Bringing elements closer together as you taper them toward a common point creates the illusion of distance perspective. Changing direction while tapering and narrowing creates the illusion of turning a corner and withdrawing into the distance. Distortion capability in your graphic production system can also be used to create additional dimensional perspective.

Textures can be created by using webbing sprays, sponge techniques, graining, smalt and marbleizing methods. Unusual paint or ink application devices such as lace, bubble-pack, plastic sandwich wrap, water bubbles, paint rollers, open weave papers or cloth, sand, cotton balls, toothbrushes, leaves from plants, crinkled paper, crushed egg shells, rice, crayons and candles and whatever else your imagination may conjure can be used to create

a wide variety of special effects.

An excellent reference for achieving hundreds of different paint effects is Jean Drysdale Green's *ArtEffects*, published by Watson-Guptill Publications, New York.

Be sure to use paints or inks that will bond well with the vinyl. Various brands are available and experimentation is encouraged. Some products will last longer than others. If long-term exposure is expected for painted graphics, compatible clear-coating products should be employed. It may also be necessary to periodically re-apply this clear-coating for maintenance purposes. In addition to their exposure-protection capabilities, some clear-coat products make vinyl more enamel-receptive (for example, Butch Anton's Sunscreen Clear). Regardless of the chemical product(s) you choose to use, test for suitability, follow manufacturer's directions, and exercise appropriate health and safety precautions.

Stenciling is another way to effectively use paint and vinyl products. Spray-mask stencil material used in conjunction with vinyl application quickly blends the two media. To block-out or protect the vinyl from paint application, application tape or mask can also be used. Computer-cut mask applied over enamel-receptive clear vinyl produces an easy-to-use paint stencil for the vinyl. This becomes an easy-to-install, painted graphic that is also easily removed down-the-road.

Modern color imaging technologies such as the Gerber EDGE™ and 3M Scotchprint™ make it possible to create multi-color, multi-dimensional, and texture-effect productions on one layer of vinyl while greatly reducing cutting, weeding, and application times. Photorealism is achievable as well. Advances are continuing in this field and vinyl graphics will continue to increase in value as durability, creative expression, and ease-of-use improves.

Advanced Vinyl Application

WHEN USING VINYL, one often faces difficult application conditions or more visually creative designs, both of which require using advanced vinyl techniques. Three important techniques — multi-component registration, damaged or contaminated graphics and detailed graphics involving dimensional perspective and paint effects — were discussed at length in the previous chapter. The handling of extreme temperatures, compound curves and corrugated surfaces, striping techniques when cutting, turning and tapering, textured or porous substrates and easy, rapid film removal are the focus of this chapter. Specialized vinyl techniques will be discussed in the next chapter.

TEMPERATURE EXTREMES

Master principle: Vinyl graphics can be installed within a broad temperature range because you control the vinyl and substrate temperatures.

A discussion of temperature extremes may seem to be an academic explanation to those who always work in the temperature-controlled environment of a signshop or garage. But sooner or later you will need to accomplish these types of applications outside the shop in less than ideal conditions.

Vinyl graphics can be installed on the hood of a black car at noon with the sun directly overhead. They can be installed on the same car in the shade on a sub-freezing day — even after you have chipped ice from the vehicle. How? By using methods for quickly cooling or heating the surface and the vinyl prior to application.

If applying vinyl in the heat use a water or alcohol rinse to cool the hot surface rapidly. (Application fluid accomplishes the same cooling action, but the evaporation process makes using such expensive fluids cost-prohibitive. Instead, use application fluid *after* you've achieved the "cool-down.") Once the surface is cool or neutral to the touch, finish the application quickly before it re-heats. Blocking the sun is also desirable; if possible, put the surface and the graphics themselves in the shade or under a tarp.

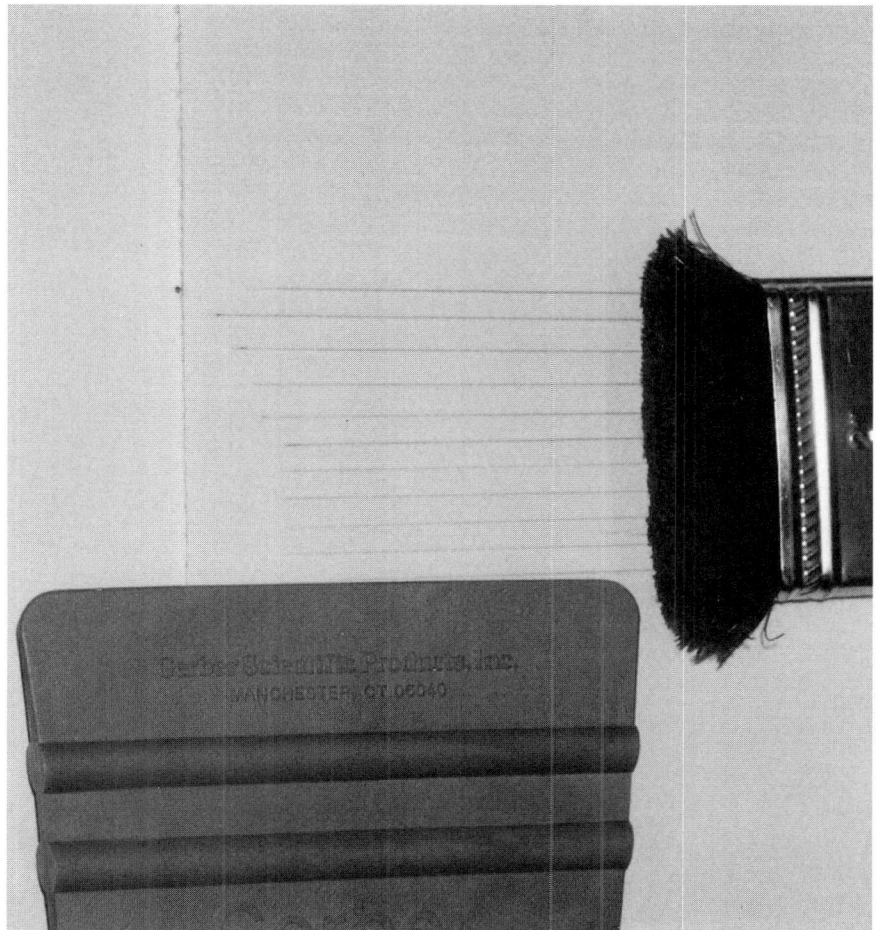

Be sure to orient your squeegee correctly when working on corrugated surfaces. Always keep the squeegee you're using parallel to the line. In contrast, move brushes (or your fingers) along the line from the center to the edges.

Conversely, cold surfaces should be moved into the sun. A heating tool should also be used to warm both the application areas and the graphics. Suitable tools include heat guns and gas-powered torches. Torches are especially useful for larger surface areas, but require more time. For overall safety, speed and spot focusing, I prefer a heat gun. If you choose to use one as well, keep it moving around the surface; don't linger in one spot and don't get too close to the surface. If you point a hot tool at anything very long, you will burn, melt or cook it. Finally, do not lay a hot tool against anything that could be damaged by the contact.

CURVES AND CORRUGATION

Master principle: High performance cast vinyl will conform to and remain on compound curves and corrugated surfaces when you use the right methods and stay within the performance capabilities of the film.

Try this experiment. You will need two samples of high-performance cast vinyl 1/2-in. wide and 6 in. long. Grab both ends of one of the sample pieces. Stretch. See how much longer you make the sample before it breaks. A sample whose temperature is cold or neutral will usually break after only 1/4-1/2 of an in.

Now warm the other sample with a heat gun or by placing it close to a hot light bulb. Gradually and continually

The stripe will lie straight as long as you stretch it tautly. Practice stretching and check your results by looking down the length of the stripe. Do not over-stretch to the point of distortion.

heating the full length of the sample will allow you to more than double its length. This demonstrates the great elongation capability of high performance cast vinyl. You should observe that the adhesive on good quality vinyl will also elongate yet remain intact; this is because of the adhesive's flow capability. Taken together, the flexibility of the vinyl and the adhesive allow you to conform high performance cast vinyl to compound curves and corrugated surfaces.

WARNING! Calendered vinyl does not perform as well or retain a stretched shape and should therefore not be used for curved and corrugated applications.

There is just one hitch to this experiment. As you stretch the vinyl, it becomes narrower. In fact, it will shrink to about 1/4-in. width. Doubling the sample's length reduces its width by half. When cutting vinyl, keep these proportions in mind and compensate for this dimensional reduction. Most simple or gentle curves can be worked with little or no addition of material; they may only require a quick trim along any edge distortion. For more extreme curves, the dimensions of the piece should be adjusted so that you have something to grab and stretch. Distortion and excess material can then be "erased" by trimming with your knife.

This technique works well for striping, but what about lettering or graphics? Occasionally, you'll need to add or piece-in material when the graphic distorts beyond your ability to re-shape it with a knife. Obviously, your graphics will be easier to re-shape if they are smaller along one axis or dimension; design with this in mind.

Designing your graphics to avoid curved or corrugated areas is an even easier way avoid facing application challenges. Or you can lay out the design — on a helmet for instance (the ultimate monster compound curve!) — with masking or fine line tape. Then apply a large piece of bulk, raw vinyl to the surface and use "pull" and heat to trim the design inside your guidelines.

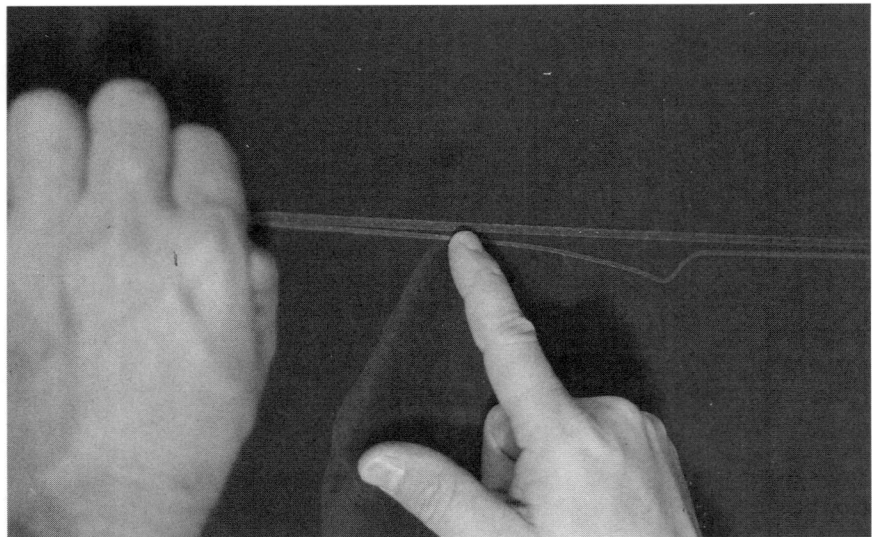

Tapering stripes is accomplished by re-lifting a stripe and closely registering it with another.

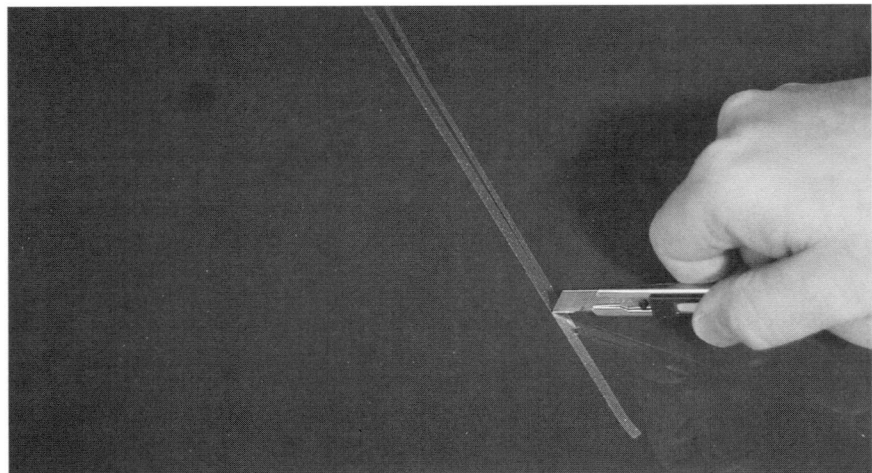

When you can cut through the vinyl without scratching the plastic, you have the "right touch." Always keep a sharp blade for cutting stripes; an Olfa™ knife works well. Balance the knife between the thumb and forefinger, with the point of the blade against the vinyl. Do not press down too hard or you'll risk cutting the substrate.

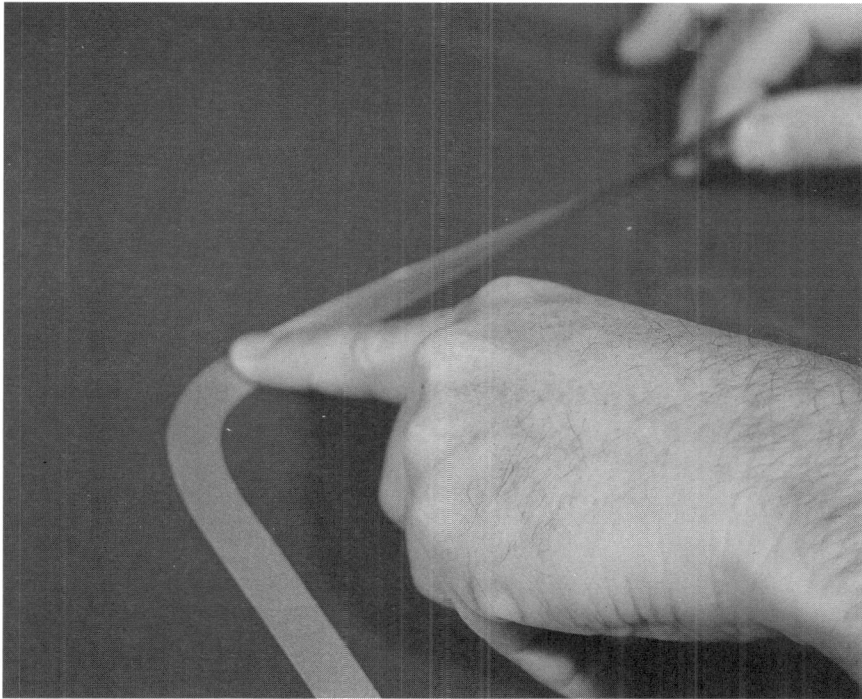

"Turning" striping involves stretching the material on the outside of the turn while pressing the inside of the turn so that wrinkles don't form. This is accomplished by pulling the stripe with one hand, and rubbing the stripe through the turn with the other (or with a squeegee). Remember: fingers are more sensitive than squeegees to the turning process.

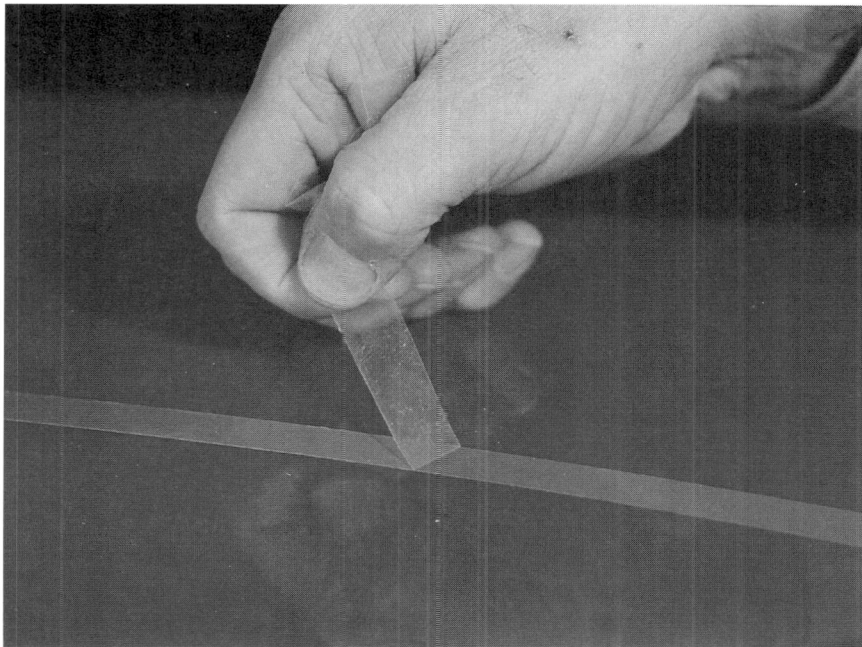

Remove any clear polyethylene mask. It has more "memory" than the vinyl and pulls the vinyl loose in the turns.

The squeegee you select will affect your ability to contend with compound curves. A flat-bladed squeegee is not suitable for this type of application. Your thumb and fingers, however, work very well. A surface-conforming squeegee (remember the chopped off paint brush?) is also suitable, if you have a dense bristle pattern and firm contact. Working the application into the proper position on a compound curve can be a real challenge; you may have to press, pull, press, snap back past the point of contact, re-press, continue to pull, stretch and squeegee. And yet you'll *still* have to use your knife to remove edge distortions and re-shape!

Corrugated truck beds can stymie the most experienced applicator. Fortunately, there is a growing trend toward smooth surface trailers. But meanwhile, when faced with this application situation . . . allow plenty of time. Corrugated surfaces require careful and proper squeegee use. The squeegee you use may be your thumb or fingers depending on the width, height, and frequency of the corrugations. If the trailer side looks like a panel of corrugated metal roofing, you will be doing a lot of finger squeegeeing!

Ribbed type trailers with raised spars — common on horse trailers — have flat panels separated by protruding ribs. Apply the graphic between the ribs if at all possible. If you must overlay one or more ribs, apply the graphic between the rips and up their sides. Bulk vinyl can be used to "cap" the ribs, and should then be trimmed to blend with your graphics. If you overlap the "cap" vinyl down the sides of the ribs, seams will be unnoticeable.

When working with any corrugated surface — even corrugated plastic yard signs — your squeegee blade should be parallel with the corrugations or flutes. Because flute seams are lower than the material face, squeegeeing across the flutes creates "valleys" of air; in-line squeegeeing prevents this bubbling. A surface-conforming squeegee works well for pressing the vinyl into such crevices. For effective squeegeeing, this orientation principle always applies: keep a squeegee parallel to the

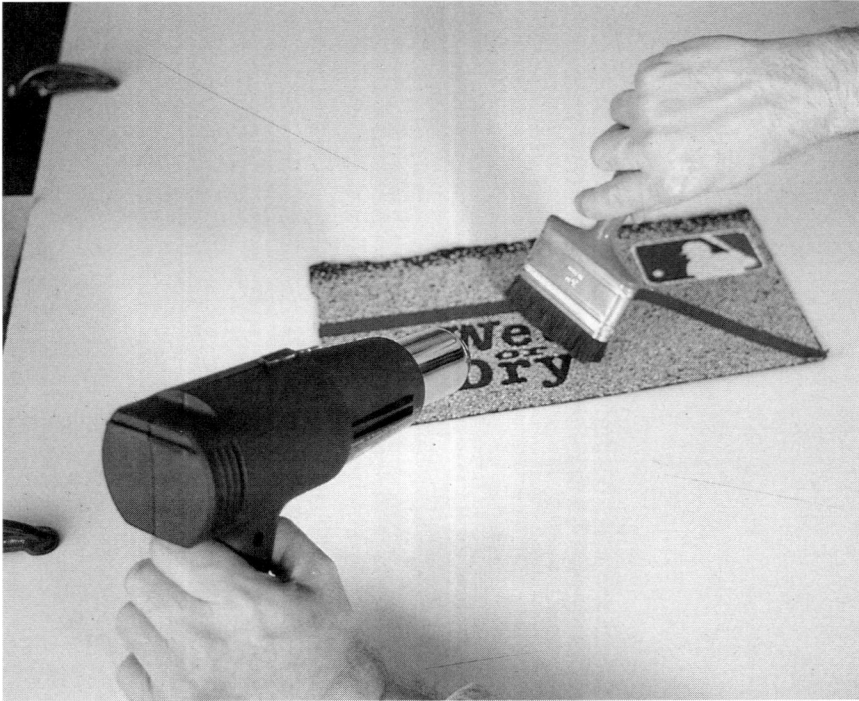

When heated, vinyl becomes more malleable. Place the vinyl in contact with the textured surface by using a surface-conforming squeegee (chopped paint brush). Work slowly until you're comfortable using a heat gun with a brush on a rough surface.

line of the corrugation, but move the brushes or fingers along the flutes to the edges of the graphic *(see photo on page 23)*.

One final point: pre-converted vinyl striping products generally have a clear polyethylene mask which conforms better to curves and corrugations than a paper mask. Pre-converted vinyl striping also retains its original dimensions with less distortion prior to mask removal.

STRIPING
Master principle: The secret to straight striping is stretch; the secret to smooth curves is "stretch and vector." Try to learn by watching and emulating a master.

Good striping requires straight lines, smooth arcs, clean radius turns and elegant tapering without damage to the substrate. These skills are properly learned from masters of striping, not from sellers of vinyl or business opportunities.

Tack one end of a vinyl stripe to a substrate. (Again, calendered vinyl can not stand up at this performance level. Use high performance cast vinyl only!) Patio doors and smooth refrigerator doors make good practice surfaces. Pull the stripe *tautly* to another point; pulling assures a straight line *(see top photo on page 24)*. Check your results by looking down the length of the stripe. Be careful not to overstretch to the point of distortion.

To accommodate the gentle arcs and curves of vehicle fenders, you need to coordinate the landing of the stripe on the surface with the rising or dropping motion of your hand. I call this technique "stretch and vector." It's a much more effective method than using your finger to rub the stripe into position; rubbing creates pivot points wherever you touch or stop, and does not allow a

smooth arcing of the stripe.

On a quality stripe product, the pressure-sensitive adhesive grabs and holds the curve as you raise or drop the stripe. If the stripe does not grab, you may need to re-prep the surface. If it still does not grab, *gently* rub the stripe onto the surface. Then snap it back off, and re-apply it using the stretch and vector method. It usually grabs after doing this because the light rubdown "activates" the adhesive, giving it more initial tack.

Tapers are made by re-lifting one stripe and closely registering it with another *(see middle photo on page 24)*. Stripes may be overlapped, but make certain they are firmly burnished together. It is usually best to overlap from the top so as to put the edge on the bottom. When pinstriping, I usually overlap the largest stripe from the top to "capture" the smaller stripe underneath. Trim the smaller stripe 1/4-1/2-in. shorter than the top stripe prior to overlapping so the end of the top stripe can directly adhere to the surface. Tapering is done correctly when inspection does not reveal where the taper started; no visible pivot point should be discernible.

Trim the ends carefully with a stainless steel Olfa™ knife. Stainless steel blades are safer on paint — especially on glass — than harder carbon blades that may scratch. Use a rounded cut to simulate paint and to avoid catching fine fibers from the synthetic chamois frequently used for detailing vehicles *(see bottom photo on page 24)*. Balance the knife between thumb and forefinger with the point of the blade against the vinyl. Do not press down. Lift the back of the knife with your remaining fingers in order to exert the very slight downforce needed to slice through the film. Be careful never to apply so much pressure that you cut or scratch the paint or other substrate. You may want to practice cutting on scrap acrylic plastic so this doesn't happen. When you can cut through the vinyl without scratching the plastic, you have the right touch. A sharp blade is a must for this procedure, so I always recommend using the snap-off Olfa knife.

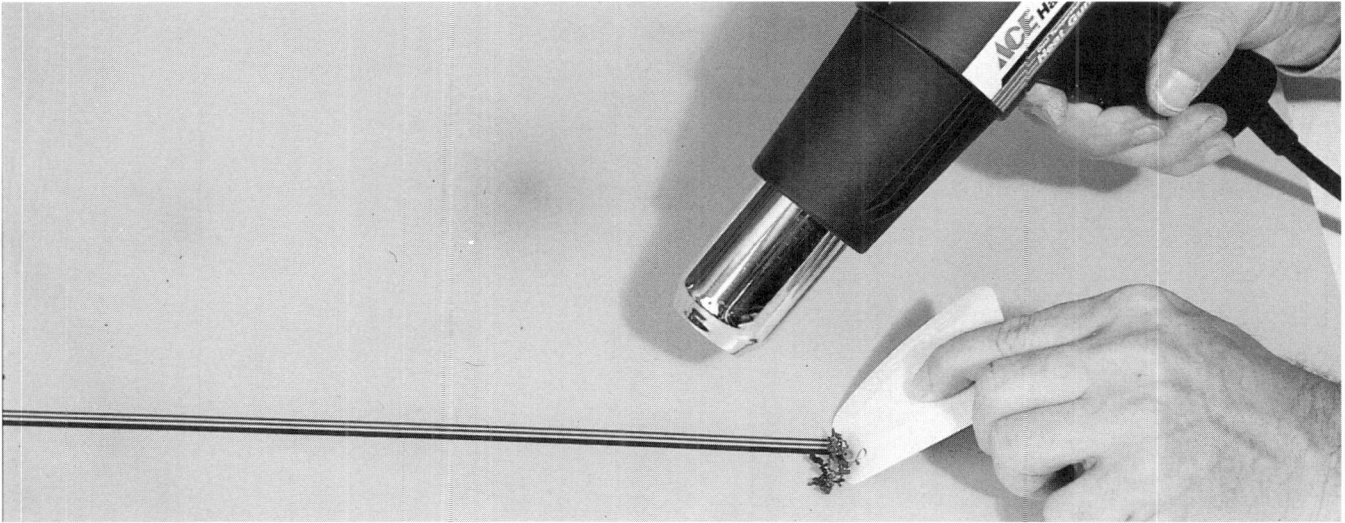

To remove vinyl that is old and fragmented, it is often necessary to employ a heat gun, heat lamp, or a gas torch. You may also need to scrape the vinyl with a tool like the "Li'l Chiseler."

"Turning" striping eliminates the wrinkles that try to bunch up. It involves pulling the stripe with one hand, while rubbing the stripe through the turn with either the fingers of your other hand or a squeegee (see top photo on page 25). Because fingers are more sensitive to the correct application of pressure than a traditional squeegee, they're your best bet. Just remember that the inside of the turn requires more pressure than the outside of the turn. And, if the turn appears crude — not smooth — snap it back past the offending point and re-do it.

Proper turning requires considerable practice to perfect. How sharply you make a turn depends on your skill and the width of the material. Start with narrow stripes and work your way up to wider ones as you improve. If your turning finger tends to grab and causes the turn to break, rub the side of your nose with your finger; your finger should then slip smoothly over the vinyl. After rubbing your nose, be sure to rub only the stripe, however. Otherwise, you'll contaminate the application surface with skin oils.

Slight distortions in a turn can be "erased" by trimming with your knife. Or, if the inside of the turn wrinkles

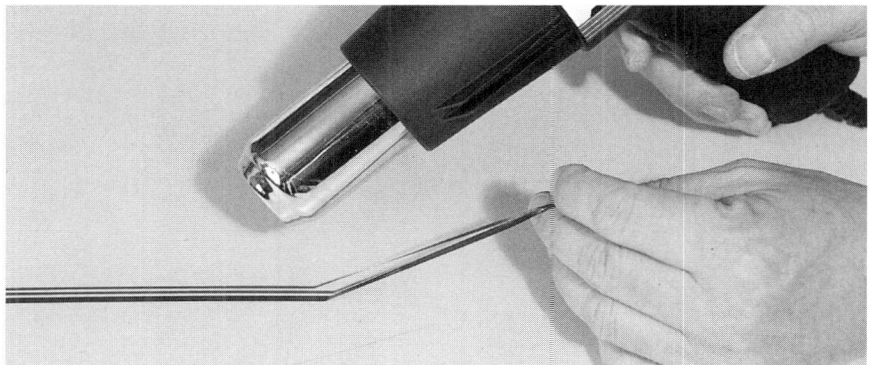

If the vinyl film is still intact, lift the film, pulling it back at a 30° angle to the surface. Doing so causes the adhesive to shear off with the vinyl. Because rubbing and scraping the adhesive won't be necessary, much adhesive removal time will be saved.

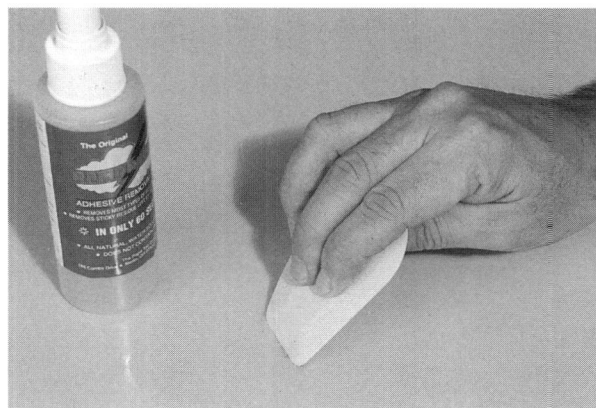

Sometimes it's necessary to remove vinyl with chemicals. Di-limonene or citrus-based adhesive removers are marketed as safer alternatives to petrochemical solvents.

Always tighten the core before using a roll of striping. Hold the core and pull the stripe tight. It's a simple process that will save a lot of grief.

The proper way to hold striping and dispense it from a roll is to hold the roll and the core in one hand. Hold the release liner with two fingers from the same hand. When you start applying, use your free hand to guide the laying of the stripe.

and you cannot make the wrinkles lie down, re-prep that area and re-apply the stripe; you may have contaminated it by handling the stripe or touching the surface. Be sure to remove any clear polyethylene mask as well. Polyethylene has more "memory" and pulls the vinyl loose in the turns. Small wrinkles in the turn can usually be removed by rubbing from the center toward the edge with the back of a fingernail.

TEXTURED SUBSTRATES

Master principle: Conformation, not adhesion, is the key issue with textured surfaces. There is actually more surface area on a textured substrate than a flat one. You just have to get down to it.

The acrylic adhesive system on a high performance, cast vinyl film is remarkable in its ability to latch onto and hold a variety of materials. I have had vinyl stick to the rubber sole of my shoe and not come off for months until I removed it. (The vinyl that is, not my shoe!) My wife has located lost graphics stuck on the bottom of the washing machine several months after I lost them. Years later . . . still there! I have seen and applied vinyl to stucco, brick and even roofing shingles, and the graphics have lasted for years. Adhesion is rarely the problem. Getting the vinyl adhesive into *contact* with the surface is the challenge.

Quite simply, the vinyl must assume the surface texture of the substrate. Apply heat to improve the vinyl's malleability *(see photo on page 26).* Then place the vinyl in contact with the textured surface by using a surface-conforming squeegee (a chopped paint brush). Work slowly until you get the hang of using a heat gun with a brush on a rough surface. Once the vinyl adheres, remove the mask gradually. If needed, apply more heat and continue to brush. Do not overheat to the point of curling the edge of the vinyl. Do hair dryers work? Yes . . . for drying your hair! But not for this! Invest in a good quality heat gun. Master Appliance™ and Dayton™ are well-known, industrial-quality heat gun suppliers. Paint stripper heat guns, readily available in hardware stores, work well and are no more expensive than good quality hair

dryers. Just be sure you don't get confused and try to dry your hair with a heat gun!

REMOVAL TECHNIQUES

Master principle: The health of the vinyl graphics industry relies on providing safe, fast, reasonably priced removal service. It can also be a very profitable.

Removing vinyl requires heat or the use of very strong chemicals. Any chemical used to remove vinyl or adhesive must be properly used and disposed. Some chemicals have been proven hazardous, while other so-called "safe" chemicals have probably not been sufficiently tested to determine long-term health effects from their usage. It is therefore advisable to err on the side of caution. Obtain manufacturer safety recommendations for proper chemical usage.

In some instances (for example, truck trailers or outside walls), a combination of chemicals and high pressure sprayers is very effective. For these removal situations, apply the chemical with a garden sprayer, give it time to work, and blast with a high-pressure sprayer. Again, properly dispose of the waste from this procedure.

Certain "repositionable" film products like Controltac™ make removal easier down the road. But beware; there are many materials that do not have this ease-of-removal built into them. In fact, many are just the opposite. With these, you need to know how to quickly pull the vinyl and remove any adhesive residue without damaging the substrate.

Because of the aforementioned health considerations, I prefer to use heat instead of chemicals when removing vinyl. Often the sun's heat on a warm day is sufficient to facilitate removal. But if the vinyl is old and fragmented, a heat gun, heat lamp or gas torch should be employed *(see the top photo on page 27).* Again, be careful when working with sources of heat — especially open flames. Get the film very warm to the

touch. You can then safely scrape the vinyl with a "Li'l Chiseler" — a pocket tool I call my "2-in. wide thumbnail." Available from Film Handler Tools, *(see their listing in the Resouce Guide on page 40),* this scraper is made from polycarbonate and does not scratch most surfaces.

If the film is still intact, lift the vinyl and pull it back at about a 30° angle to the surface *(see the middle photo on page 27).* This method causes the adhesive to shear off with the vinyl and will save you much removal time. Further, it prevents surface marring caused by chemicals, towels and scrapers. A combination of two-parts MEK (methyl ethyl ketone) and one-part xylene makes a fast and effective chemical adhesive remover. Just be sure to exercise appropriate caution in its use. Di-limonene or citrus-based adhesive removers are marketed as safer alternatives to petrochemical solvents.

Rotary rubber erasers and self-destructive pads that mount to high-torque drills are sold for removing vinyl and adhesive. Used properly, they are safe and effective on most substrates. I've found, however, that they are slower than my heat gun/ correct pull angle/"Li'l Chiseler"/ chemical adhesive remover method.

It is quite likely that new chemical alternatives and easier-to-remove vinyls and adhesive systems will be invented. In the meantime, our industry must accept the responsibility to offer removal service to those who have purchased and enjoyed our vinyl graphics products in years past. We must also remove inferior applications at a reasonable cost, or if we originally installed the offending product, free-of-charge. Suitable removal tools and methods exist; we should practice skillfully using them.

Master principle:
Advanced performance and superior results are expected from "masters of the craft." Always remember that a master is — first and foremost — a student. Never stop learning new and better ways to master the craft.

Specialized Vinyl Application

THIS FINAL CHAPTER discusses specialized application considerations: translucent and retro-reflective films; goldleaf films; painting, airbrushing and color imaging; and heat transfer graphics.

TRANSLUCENT AND RETRO-REFLECTIVE FILMS

Master principle: Adjust your handling of specialized films to compensate for their unique characteristics.

Circumstances sometimes dictate the use of specialized film. Your vinyl graphics may, for example, need to be visible at night. This desired visibility is obtained by either back-lighting the graphics or by front-lighting them with a source light.

In the first situation, use translucent films on back-lit clear or translucent substrates. Doing so assures the transmittal of uniform color, day or night. Opaque film can be combined with this type of production and used as block-out film — film that appears one color during the day, yet seems black at night. By using diffuser films such as Scotchcal™ Series 3635-30 or Series 3635-70, clear substrates can be made translucent. If you need maximum graphic protection for the face of the sign, you can use GPS (Scotchcal™ Series 3640-114 HA film), Rexcal 6000 2-mil cast, fluoropolymer film, or a 1-mil cast, fluoropolymer film available from SignGold Corp. 3M's excellent "Tips for Translucents" guide offers additional suggestions and information for this application situations, and can be obtained by calling (800) 328-3908.

Some fundamental translucent graphic tips include:

1. When a customer wants a matte finish, use first-surface application. The image and background color — if used — should be applied to the front side of the substrate (which is usually a diffuse white surface). The image should be cut to be right-reading.

2. For a glossy finish or added graphic protection, use second-surface application. The image and optional background color should be applied to the back side of a clear, rigid substrate. The images should be cut in reverse, and colors should be applied in

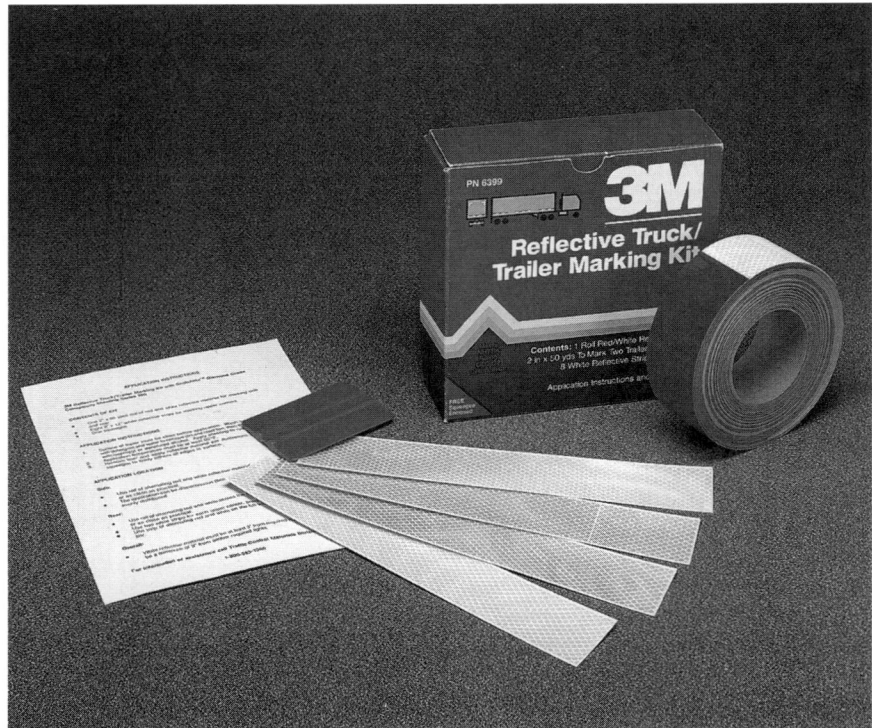

Reflective truck/trailer marking kits are available through 3M.

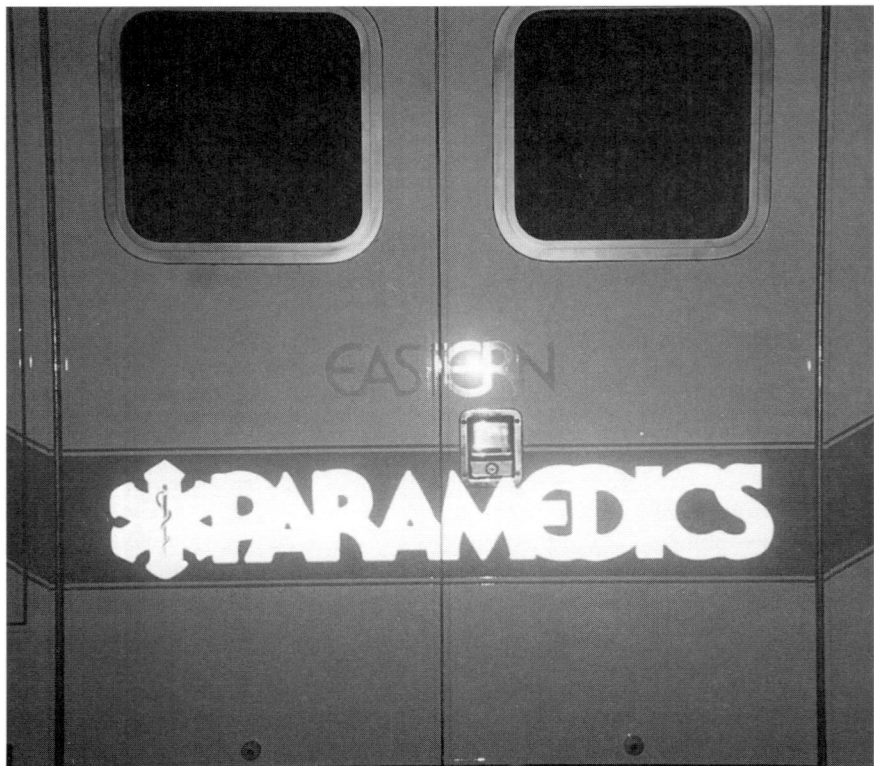

Graphics with nighttime visibility can save lives.

the opposite order of first-surface applications.

3. Because polycarbonate substrates absorb moisture, they can outgas and form bubbles. Adding layers of film increases this bubbling potential. Follow the substrate manufacturer's recommendations for drying and sealing substrates prior to film application. Also, apply manufacturer-recommended sealants to both sides of polycarbonate substrates to prevent outgassing, panel warp and distortion.

4. Prep surface with water and tar, wax, grease, and silicone remover. Then, them dry before the solvent evaporates. Wiping with alcohol or wipe a dryer anti-static sheet helps discharge static pockets.

5. Use wet application methods when applying translucent films. As always, squeegee properly: Move from the center to the edges with firm, overlapping strokes.

6. Avoid seaming; try to use whole sections of film. If overlapping films is necessary, however, use a 1/32-in. overlap to minimize the seam and prevent potential leaks from weathering. Should two or more pieces of the same color film need to be seamed into a continuous band, use film from the same roll or lot. To assure a uniform appearance, "swing" matching edges to meet each other.

7. Put dark color films over light colors and overlap them 1/32-1/16 in. to compensate for registration errors. The darker overlap helps frame the lighter color.

8. Internal lamps may show on the face of the production as streaks, hot spots or bright outlines. Eliminate or reduce this undesirable effect by applying diffuser film to the back of the face. Deeper cabinets or multiple layers may be required as well.

Using light-reflecting film is another way to give graphics nighttime visibility. This film is more properly referred to as retro-reflective film since the film returns light to its source, rather than reflecting the light in the opposite direction. When applied to signs and vehicles, retro-reflective film does much more than provide around-the-clock visibility; it saves lives and prevents property damage.

Applying the genuine gold, self-adhesive film pictured here is much easier to learn than hand-gilding. Another advantage to this type of film is the ease with which it can be cut, installed and maintained.

Retro-reflective film's light-directing capability comes from either an intense accumulation of micro-fine glass beads or from an angular prism effect precisely etched onto its surface. To block translucency and to enhance color intensity and reflectivity, retro-reflective film usually has white or silver pigment added to its adhesive system. Because this construction makes the film heavy, it tends to sag; installing in smaller lengths (especially when striping) is advised. Heat should be avoided except when spot-softening around rivet heads. Also, it is better to install this film using dry application methods. Use good squeegee techniques and remove bubbles with the puncture-and-push method.

GENUINE GOLDLEAF FILM

Master principle: Goldleaf, whether hand- or pre-assembled, comprises an adhesive system, a layer of fine gold and a protective surface coating.

One of the most advanced or specialized signmaking methods is goldleaf. It can take many years of dedicated practice to achieve artistic results with goldleaf — results

that look great and last many years.

By using a genuine gold, self-adhesive film, however, this learning curve can be significantly shortened, artistic results can be speedily produced, and the life of the finished production can be greatly enhanced. At the same time, maintenance procedures can be streamlined if the protective surface coating resists pollution and solvents. Fluoropolymer surface coatings make the film graffiti-proof and fade-resistant.

Films of this caliber are available in the marketplace and can easily be hand- or computer-cut. First-surface finishes such as matte, engine turn, and special grain patterns are offered, as are mirror- and matte-second-surface films. Pre-converted pinstriping is also available, and can be used to border signs or accent vehicles. Real gold requires no edge sealing and fluoropolymer coating requires no waxing. Ten- to 14-year acrylic adhesive systems allow you to offer long warranty coverage for your productions.

The high-perceived value of real gold and silver, coupled with the convenience of speedy delivery, enable you to charge as much for these productions as for hand applied metal.

Recent advances in vinyl technology allow it to be air-brushed. Also, it is now possible to automate airbrush effects by using a plotter that both cuts and sprays.

Special effects can be achieved on vinyl by brushing, rolling, sponging, spattering, texturing, stamping, etc. Shown here is a webbing process that is also possible.

Remember, it is poor marketing to diminish the value of your productions or those of other skilled craftspeople.

PAINTS, COATINGS AND FINISHES
Master principle: When adding color, shading or texture to vinyl, use durable, compatible paints, inks and clearcoats.

Recent advances in paints, inks, and clearcoat products make it possible to create productions that incorporate mixed media. You can easily combine vinyl's durability and ease of production/application with the inexpensive special effect capabilities of paint and airbrushing. By using a plotter that both cuts and sprays, it is even possible to automate airbrush activity (*see photo at top left*). More expensive automated painting systems also work well with vinyl.

Special effects are achieved with paint on vinyl by brushing, rolling, sponging, spattering, webbing, texturing, marbleizing, water bubbling,

Paint on enamel-receptive, clear vinyl is easy to produce in the shop and install on-site.

Graphic design by "Crazy Jack" Willis

Paints and inks should have flexibility and elongation capabilities that approximate those of the vinyl. This will assure that colors do not distort when the film has to stretch over a compound curve, textured or flexible substrate.

The Gerber Edge™ directly places outdoor-durable color on vinyl and creates process-color, photo-realistic reproductions or originals that can be contour-cut.

crumpling, stenciling, solvent washing, screening, pressing, stamping, rubbing, masking, and resisting. In fact, with the proper paint, any artistic, creative effect used by painters of fine art can likewise be used on vinyl. If you study these effects and refer to the book *Professional Painted Finishes* by Ina Brosseau Marx, Allen Marx and Robert Marx, (the principles of The Finishing School — their book is available from ST Publications), you will be able to achieve striking results.

So that the colors do not distort if the film has to stretch over a textured substrate, compound curve, or flexible substrate, the paint or ink you use needs to approximate vinyl's flexibility, durability and elongation capability. These requirements should help you select appropriate paints and inks. And remember: If long-term durability is required, your painted graphic should be clear-coated. Certain automotive urethanes — those that have catalysts mixed with them — are good options.

Color imaging technologies are emerging for use with vinyl. Electrostatic, thermal, and ink jet color applications have been developed (or are being developed) as alternatives to hand-applied color *(see photo at bottom left)*. The Gerber Edge™, for instance, directly places outdoor-durable color on vinyl. The Edge creates process-color, photo-realistic reproductions and originals, both of which can be contour-cut. Very fine details — details that would be impossible to weed — can be printed *(see photos on page 34)*. ScotchPrint™ indirectly transfers color to vinyl, and can be laminated to extend its outdoor durability. Ink jet printers have not yet been able to achieve outdoor-durable colors. Their productions are therefore limited primarily to indoor applications where little, if any, UV action is present.

Advancements are expected for all these systems as time goes on. Similarly, the demand for color effects should also escalate. Right now, the most improvement is not needed technologically, however; rather, strides need to be made in signshops' marketing of their color capabilities.

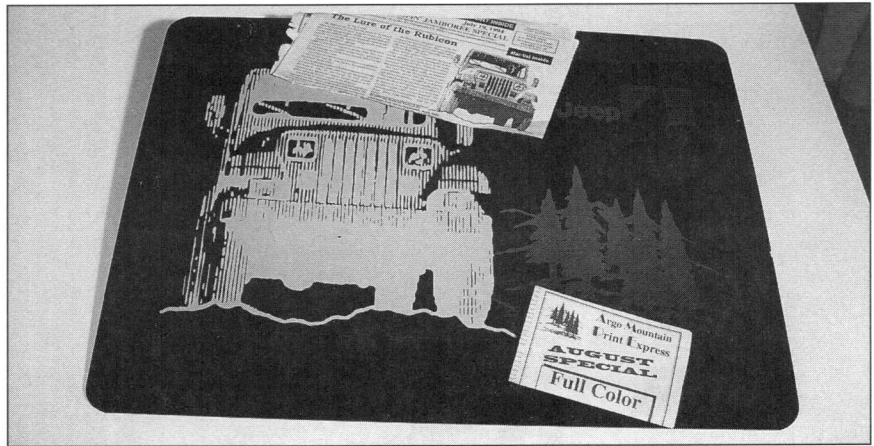

Very fine details can be printed on vinyl, even details that would have been impossible to weed.

Shops need to make full use of specialty vinyls to create shadows, textures and graduated fade effects.

One film currently available — True Shadow™ by Universal Products — changes the color value of a background. In this way, it is much like the real shadow a three-dimensional object would cast on a surface. Still other vinyls offer graduated color, textured, marbleized or spattered effects. Holographic films that break light into different patterns of colorful prismatic projections are also exciting alternatives. Be aware though, that many holographic films are metalized polyester and have limited outdoor durability.

To stay at the forefront of your field, constantly update your files with new product information. Keeping this information at-hand should result in fresh, new ways to present your work.

HEAT TRANSFER GRAPHICS

Master principle: There are many ways to bring added value and variety to your vinyl graphic productions.

In addition to pressure-sensitive adhesive systems, there are also heat-sensitive systems you can use. These make it possible to apply graphics to diverse substrates, including shirts, hats, car seats and horse blankets. Such applications complement graphics created on signs and vehicles. Using heat transfers, you can personalize your customers' belongings, increasing their "pride-of-ownership value." Company logos can also be generated then heat-transferred to cloth surfaces. Similarly, sublimation printers can make photo-realistic transfers for wearables, mugs, and other promotional tools. These options will prove attractive for your customers; they can enhance their advertising efforts by hiring you to put their company's name in front of more viewers. You may also gain business by graphically "decorating" your customer's business possessions with his/her company's name and logo.

Heat transfers can be produced in four major materials: thermal wax transfers, electro-static ink transfers, hot-split plastisol, and heat transfer flock. The first two are generally produced on special sublimation printers

Vinyl makes a striking addition to dimensional wood signage.

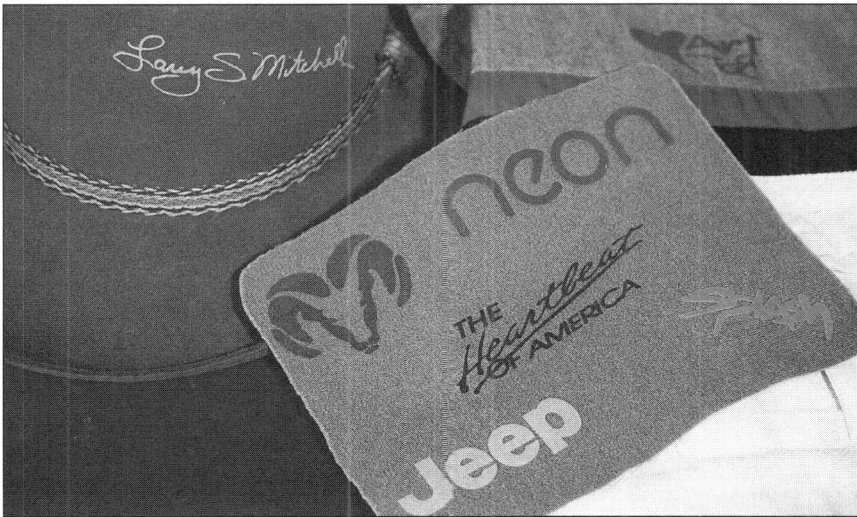

Art-A-Tac™ is the first and only patent-pending graphics application system that makes on-site installation of heat transfer graphics possible.

A master of a craft is, first and foremost, a student. Participate regularly in educational trade events and acquire all the educational tools you can find.

or by producers using screen production. These transfers are usually multi-color and complex designs are possible. The last two are usually hand-, die-, or computer-generated and are for simpler, single color designs. Multiple colors can still be achieved by registering additional single colors. An added advantage of heat transfer flock is that it looks and feels like cloth. All these media have been designed for long-term durability, even when laundered regularly.

The traditional application tool for heat transfers is a heat press. Different types of presses exist for various articles of clothing. A certain type of press, for example, is used for shirts and jackets, while a different press is used for hats. Still another type of press is used for cups with a specially prepared receptive surface.

Art-A-Tac™ is the first and only patent-pending, *portable* graphics application system for installing heat transfers *(see photo on page 35)*. It enables easy, *on-site application* of graphics; the substrate need not be removed from its location and taken to an in-shop press. With this tool, for example, graphics can be applied to a vehicle's interior, without removing any upholstery cloth from the car. By coordinating exterior and interior graphics in this way, you become a truly full-service graphics installer. Subsequently, the value of your services is enhanced.

MASTERY OF CRAFT

Master principle: Mastery is a path, not a destination. A master is, first and foremost, a student. Frustration inevitably occurs when a student hits a plateau; however, this is where most learning occurs. A true master perseveres through such plateaus and continues to climb.

By now you have come to understand that there are really no limits to what can be achieved with vinyl graphics. The only limits that exist are those you establish in your mind.

You have seen that vinyl can be combined in innumerable ways with other products, including paint, ink, goldleaf, heat transfers and dimensional signage. It can be installed on nearly any substrate, in nearly any environmental situation. If I had a good ship and a space suit, I would . . . .

Vinyl will literally go over rocks, under water and through dust. It is hindered only by those who do not educate themselves on its proper use or those who choose to use vinyl with inferior qualities. Remember, use the best, not the cheapest! Give your clients long-term value by offering excellent productions — not just cheap prices. Contribute to the strength of your industry by being the best you can be and by helping your competitor improve, too. Shake off pricing insecurity and use a published pricing authority like the *Official Sign Contractors' Pricing Guide* (available from ST Publications).

Finally, keep your eyes and ears tuned to your trade. Regularly participate in trade seminars and acquire all the educational tools *(see photo at left)* you can find.

Vinyl Graphics *Gallery*

MAIL CALL·USA

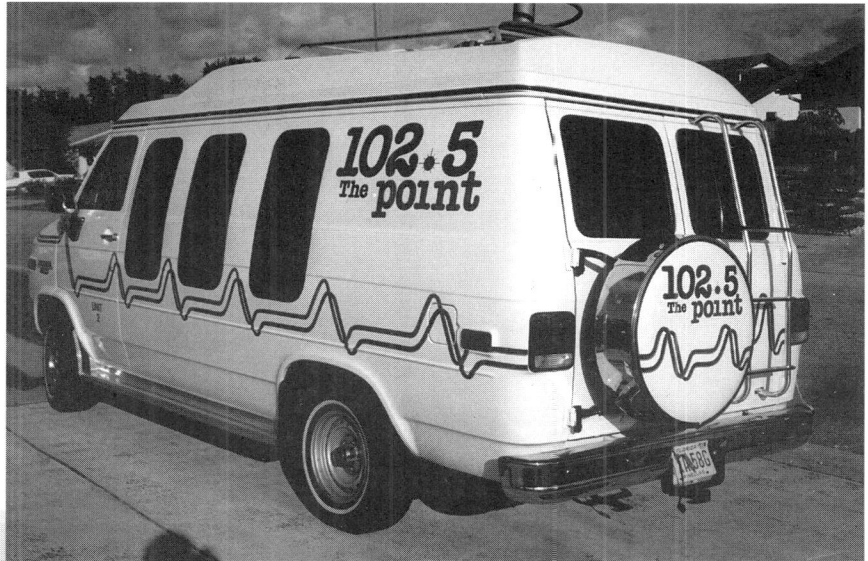

Vinyl Products Resource List

The following resource list should provide a very good starting point for anyone who wants to set up a vinyl shop. For additional manufacturers and suppliers of vinyl products and services, check *Signs of the Times* Buyers' Guide, published in January.

Vinyl Films

Arlon Adhesives and Film Div.
2811 S. Harbor Blvd.
Santa Ana, CA 92704
Ph: (800) 540-2811 (in CA)
Ph: (800) 854-0361 (other)
Fax: (714) 540-7190

Avery Dennison Marking &
Promotional Films Div.
250 Chester St.
Painesville, OH 44077
Ph: (216) 639-3000
Fax: (216) 639-3759

Flexcon Co., Inc.
Flexcon Industrial Park
Spencer, MA 01562
Ph: (508) 885-3973
Fax: (508) 885-8400

MacTac
4560 Darrow Rd.
Stow, OH 44224
Ph: (216) 688-1111
Fax: (216) 688-2540

3M Commercial Graphics Div.
3M Center Bldg. 220-6W-06
St. Paul, MN 55144
Phone: (612) 733-1017
Fax: (612) 736-4233

Rexham Decorative
P.O. Box 800
Lancaster, SC 29721
Ph: (803) 285-4620

Ritrama Duramark
341 Eddy Rd.
Cleveland, OH 44108
Ph: (216) 851-2300
Fax: (216) 851-1938

Additional Vinyl Products

Arlon Adhesives and Films
2811 S. Harbor
P.O. Box 5260
Santa Ana, CA 92704
Ph: (714) 540-0361
Striping Products

Exciter's Graphics Supply
11555 D Ave.
Auburn, CA 95603
Ph: (916) 823-5197
Ph: (800) 886-5166
Fax: (916) 823-8239
Vinyl Tech Vinyl Coating
Paints

Filmhandler
2000 Yolande Ave.
Lincoln, NE 68521
Ph: (402) 474-1243
Ph: (800) 336-3971
Fax: (402) 474-1361
Stainless Steel NT and
OLFA knives and blades,
Li'l Chiselers

Gerber Scientific Products, Inc.
151 Batson Drive
Manchester, CT 06040
Ph: (203) 643-1515
Fax: (203) 645-5645
Graphic design and
production hardware
Software and materials
Gerber EDGE™ vinyl printer

GridView, Ltd.
4150 Industrial Drive
St. Peters, MO 63376
Ph: (800) 724-4743
Fax: (314) 926-7510
GridView Lettering and
Layout Projection Guide

3M Automotive Trades Div.
3M Center Bldg. 223-6N-01
St. Paul, MN 55144
Ph: (800) 364-3577
Striping products

Rapid Tac
186 Combs Dr.
Merlin, OR 97532
Ph: (800) 350-7751
Fax: (503) 474-9447

SpeedPress Tool Co.
11404 Sorrento Valley Rd. #111
San Diego, CA 92121
Ph: (800) 647-7446
Fax: (619) 558-0587
SpeedPress Tool

Software

Computer Aided Sign Making Products

Alpha Merics Corp
4420 Shopping Lane
Simi Valley, CA 93063
Ph: (805) 520-3664
Fax. (805) 520-3665
Color-output product:
Spectrum 5248 and
Spectrum 5290

American Small Business
Computers
1 American Way
Pryor, OK 74361
Ph. (918) 825-7555
Fax: (918) 825-6359
CAS Software: Vinyl CAD
Professional Signmaking
software

Amiable Technologies
Scott Plaza Two, Suite 625
Philadelphia, PA 19113
Ph: (610) 521-6300
Fax: (610) 521-0111
CAS Software, CAS Bridge
Software

Anagraph, Inc.
3100 Pullman St.
Costa Mesa, CA 92626
Ph: (714) 540-2400
Fax: (714) 966-2400
CAS software and bridge
software

Aries Graphics Intl.
5963 LaPlace Ct., Suite 110
Carlsbad, CA 92008
Ph: (800) 294-7273
Fax: (619) 929-0234
Sign Wizard signmaking
machine and compatible
software

Autogram Intl.
c/o Signprinters
1486 Max Dr.
Tallahasee, FL 32303
Ph: (904) 575-3828
Fax: (904) 575-4828
CAS software

Beacon Graphics Systems
10 County Line Rd., Suite 24
Somerville, NJ 08876
Ph: (800) 762-9205
Fax: (908) 231-8943
CAS software

Belcom Corp.
3135 Madison St.
Bellwood, IL 60104
Fax: (708) 544-5607
Color output product

Cactus
17 Industrial Rd.
Fairfield, NJ 07004
Ph: (201) 575-8810
Fax: (201) 575-5512
Color output product

Cadlink Technology Corp.
2440 Don Reid Dr., Suite 100
Ottawa, ON K1H 8H5
Canada
Ph: (800) 545-9581
Fax: (613) 247-1488

Calcomp
2411 West LaPalma Ave.
Anaheim, CA 92801
Ph: (800) 932-1212
Fax: (714) 821-2832
Color output product

Converter Solutions
Koberesteig 6
Berlin, 13156
GERMANY
Ph: 49 30 4827107
Fax: 49 30 4559977
CAS software, bridge software

Cybersign Ltd. Inc.
196 Boston Ave., Suite 2000
Medford, MA 02155
Ph: (617) 391-3100
Fax: (617) 393-0931
CAS software, bridge software

Encad
6059 Cornerstone Ct. West
San Diego, CA 92121
Ph: (619) 452-0882
Fax: (619) 452-0891
Color output product

Gerber Scientific Products
151 Batson Dr.
Manchester, CT 06040
Ph: (800) 222-7446
Fax: (203) 645-2479
CAS software and color
output product

Infographic Technologies, Inc.
250 Williams St.
Atlanta, GA 30303
Ph: (404) 523-4944
Fax: (404) 523-4882
Color output product

Lasermaster Corp.
6900 Shady Oak Rd.
Eden Prairie, MN 55344
Ph: (800) 688-8342
Fax: (612) 944-1244
Color output product

3M Co. Commercial
Graphics Div.
3M Center Bldg. 220-6W-06
St. Paul, MN 55144
Ph: (800) 328-3908
Fax: (612) 736-4233
Color output product:
Scotchprint electronic graphic
system

Metromedia Technologies
1320 N. Wilton Place
Los Angeles, CA 90028
Ph: (213) 856-6500
Fax: (213) 469-0843
Large scale digital imaging

Procut USA
3186 Airway Ave.
Costa Mesa, CA 92626
(714) 5409-7750
Fax: (714) 540-7556
CAS bridge software

Raster Graphics, Inc.
3025 Orchard Pkwy
San Jose, CA 95134
Ph: (800) 441-4788
Fax: (408) 232-4100
Color output product

Rocky Mountain Software
9739-63 Ave.
Edmonton, AB T6E 0G7
Canada
Ph: (403) 439-3303
Fax: (403) 439-3409
CAS bridge software

Scanvec, Inc.
155 West St.
Wilmington, MA 01887
Ph: (800) 866-6227
Fax: (508) 694-9482
CAS software, bridge software

Sign Equipment Engineering
P.O. Box 6188
Bellevue, WA 98008
Ph: (206) 747-0693
Fax: (206) 562-3017
CAS software, bridge software

Sign Max Enterprises, Inc.
3705 Tricentenaire Blvd.
Montreal, QC H1B 5W3
Canada
Ph: (514) 644-3177
Fax: (514) 644-3173

Signtech USA, Ltd.
4669 Hwy. 90 West
San Antonio, TX 78237
Ph: (800) 353-9322
Fax: (210) 436-5711
Color output product

Softeam
3000 Chestnut Ave.,
Suite 108-A
Baltimore, MD 21211
Ph: (800) 305-8326
Fax: (410) 243-1259
CAS software, bridge software

Solustan, Inc.
165 Chestnut St. #200
Needham, MA 02192
Ph: (617) 449-7666
Fax: (800) 666-8789
CAS software, bridge software

Summagraphic
8500 Cameron Rd.
Austin, TX 78754
Ph: (800) 337-8662
Fax: (512) 873-1329
Color imaging product

Symbol Graphics
1047 W. 6th St.
Corona, CA 91720
Ph: (909) 736-4040
Fax: (909) 737-0652
CAS software

URW
4 Manchester St.
Nashua, NH 03060
Ph. (800) 229-8791
Fax: (603) 882-7210
CAS software

Visual Edge Technology, Inc.
306 Potrero Ave.
Sunnyvale, CA 94086
Ph: (408) 245-1100
Fax: (408) 245-1107
Color output product

Vutek, Inc.
P.O. Box 1546
Meredith, NH 03253
Ph: (603) 279-4635
Fax: (603) 279-6191
Color output product

Hardware and Cutting Plotters

Accupro Inc.
1011 Highway 22
W. Bldg. C, Box 8
Phillipsburg, NJ 08865
Ph: (908) 454-5998
Fax: (908) 454-1957

Allen Datagraph, Inc.
2 Industrial Way
Salem, NH 03079
Ph: (800) 258-6360
Fax: (603) 893-9042

Anagraphic, Inc.
3100 Pullman St.
Costa Mesa, CA 92626
Ph: (800) 942-4270
Fax: (714) 966-2400

Euro Tech Corp.
14823 E. Hindsdale Ave.
Englewood, CO 80112
Ph: (303) 690-9000
Fax: (303) 690-9010

Gerber Scientific Products
151 Batson Dr.
Manchester, CT 06040
Ph: (800) 222-7446
Fax: (203) 290-5794

Ioline Corp.
12020 113 Ave. NE
P.O. Box 97095
Kirkland, WA 98034
Ph: (800) 598-0029
Fax: (206) 823-8898

Mimaki Engineering Co. Ltd.
5-9-41 Kitashinagawa
Siniagawa-Ku
Tokyo 141
JAPAN
Ph: 81-3-5420-8671
Fax: 81-3-5420-8688

Mutoh America, Inc.
3007 E. Chambers St.
Phoenix, AZ 85040
Ph: (800) 445-8782
Fax: (602) 276-9007

Newing-Hall, Inc.
2019 Monroe St.
Toledo, OH 43624
Ph: (800) 521-2615
Fax: (800) 435-7131

New Hermes, Inc.
2200 Northmont Pkwy.
Duluth, GA 30136
Ph: (800) 843-7337
Fax: (800) 533-7637

Roland Digital Corp.
1961 McGaw Ave.
Irvine, CA 92714
Ph: (714) 975-0560
Fax: (714) 975-0569

Summagraphics Corp.
8500 Cameron Rd.
Austin, TX 78754
Ph: (800) 444-3245
Fax: (512) 835-1916

Vinyl Technologies
2 Omega Way
Littleton, MA 01460
Ph: (800) 836-8983
Fax: (508) 952-6036

Western Graphtec, Inc.
11 Vanderbilt
Irvine, CA 92718
Ph: (800) 654-7568
Fax: (714) 855-0895

Striping Machines

S. B. Beugler Co.
3667 Tracy St.
Los Angeles, CA 90039
Ph: (213) 664-2195
Fax: (213) 664-7757

Newstripe, Inc.
1700 Jasper St.
Aurora, CO 80011
Ph: (303) 364-7786
Fax: (303) 364-7796

Tape

Anchor Continental, Inc.
2000 S. Beltline Blvd.
Columbia, SC 29205
Ph: (800) 845-2331
Fax: (800) 462-1293

C.P.F. A Division of
Courtaulds Coatings
P.O. Box 6369
5300 W. 5th Ave.
Gary IN 46406
Ph: (219) 949-1684
Fax: (219) 949-1612

The Exciters
11555 D. Ave.
Auburn, CA 95603
Ph: (916) 823-6241
Fax: (916) 823-8239

Gregory, Inc.
200 S. Regler St.
P.O. Box 410
Buhler, KS 67522
Ph: (316) 543-6657
Fax: (316) 543-2690

ST Publications
Books and Magazines

Signs of the Times
ST Publications, Inc.
407 Gilbert Ave.
Cincinnati, OH 45202
Ph: (513) 421-2050
(800) 421-1321 (subscriptions)
Fax: (513) 421-5144
Larry Mitchell's monthly
"Vinyl Graphics" column;
Features and special issues on
vinyl signmaking and graphics

Signs of the Times en español
ST Publications, Inc.
407 Gilbert Ave.
Cincinnati, OH 45202
Ph: (513) 421-2050 (English)
Tel: (513) 421-1257 (Spanish)
Fax: (513) 421-5144
Features and special issues on
vinyl signmaking and graphics
published in Spanish

Signs and Screen
ST Publications, Inc.
407 Gilbert Ave.
Cincinnati, OH 45202
Ph: (513) 421-2050
Fax: (513) 421-5144
Features and special issues on
vinyl signmaking and graphics
published in Portuguese

ST Publications Book Div.
407 Gilbert Ave.
Cincinnati, OH 45202
Ph: (513) 421-2050
(800) 925-1110 (orders)
Fax: (513) 421-5144
Books on vinyl graphics and
signmaking; Also publishes
books on screen printing and
visual merchandising/store
design

Read Larry Mitchell's "Vinyl Graphics" column every month in

SIGNS OF THE TIMES

For subscription information or a sample copy, call 1-800-421-1321 or fax (513) 421-5144
Visit SIGNS of the Times on the world-wide web: http://www.signweb.com/st

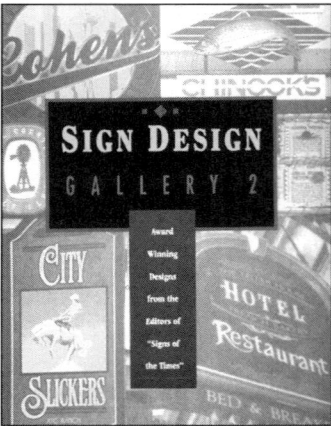

Sign Design Gallery 2

More than 300 full-color photos feature the cutting edge in sign design, both commercial and electric. Culled from *Signs of the Times* contest winners, these are the latest and very best in illuminated signs, carved signs, hanging, freestanding, wall- and post-mounted signs, glass signs, entry monuments and architectural sign systems. Brief captions offer information on the designers and fabricators, the construction materials and techniques.
Hardcover, 9 x 12, 160 pages
Order No. 55
$39.95

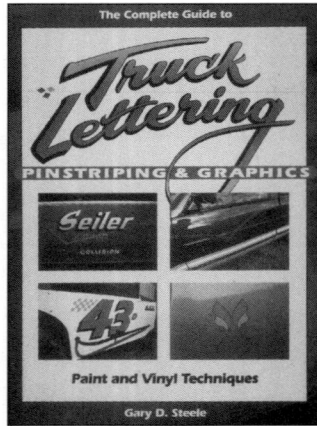

The Complete Guide to Truck Lettering

Everything you need to know about truck lettering in one highly readable, copiously illustrated book. More than 250 full-color photos take you step-by-step through the lettering process:
• Designing the job
• Conditions and location
• Vinyl lettering
Geared primarily for lettering with paint, this book is also useful to vinyl shops who want to get into brush lettering as well as vinyl.
Softcover, 8 1/2 x 11, 165 pages
Order No. 41
$29.95

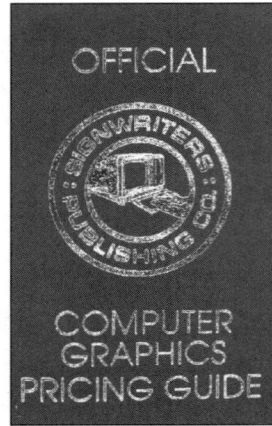

Computer Vinyl Graphics Pricing Guide

The pricing guide for banners, boat lettering, bulletin boards, installation of signs, interior (architectural) signs, magnetic signs, menu signs, pinstriping, plywood signs, race car lettering, repainted signs, showcards, vehicle lettering, window lettering and wood signs.
Softcover, 3 x 5
40 pages
Order No. 175
$7.50

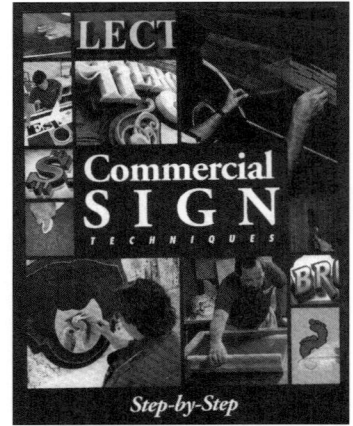

Commercial Sign Techniques

This book covers the same techniques as *Vinyl Graphics How-to*, but it features them in full-color photos. It also takes the reader step-by-step through the techniques of pinstriping with paint, banner making, airbrush sign painting, making wood signs, faux finishing and screen printing signs. In all, more than 250 full-color photos show the world's leading signmaking experts fabricating the kinds of signs commercial signshops make every day.
Hardcover, 9 x 12, 144 pages
Order No. 50
$39.95

Name _____

Company _____

Address _____

City/State/Zip _____

Phone /Fax _____

☐ Check   ☐ Visa   ☐ MC   ☐ AmEx

Card Number _____

Expiration Date _____

Signature _____

Credit card orders call toll free 1-800-925-1110
Fax this completed form to (513) 421-5144

Qty	Title	Order No.	Price
____	**Sign Design Gallery 2**	**(55)**	39.95
____	**Complete Truck Lettering**	**(41)**	29.95
____	**Computer Graphics Pricing**	**(175)**	7.50
____	**Commercial Sign Tech.**	**(50)**	39.95

Return by mail with check or money order (U.S. funds) to:
ST Publications Book Division
407 Gilbert Ave., Cincinnati, OH 45202   (VGB4)

Add $4.00 for UPS shipping for the first book and $2.00 for each additional book (U.S. delivery). Ohio residents please add 5.5% sales tax. Payment must accompany all orders. Satisfaction guaranteed. Book(s) may be returned within 15 days for a full refund (excluding shipping). Prices subject to change. Most orders shipped within 3-5 days of receiving order. Please allow up to 2-3 weeks for delivery.